101
AMAZING
THINGS
ABOUT
Christmas

HARVEST HOUSE PUBLISHERS
EUGENE, OREGON

Design by Peter Gloege | LOOK Design Studio
Cover images: © chipstudio/iStock (nativity silhouettes); Lanako/
    Shutterstock (texture); Rvika/Shutterstock (cityscape); AnyaPL/
    Shutterstock (santa's sleigh); Feliche Vero/Shutterstock (snowflakes)
Interior images: Lightstock/Shutterstock

Each of these 101 amazing things was carefully researched in the
creation of this book. If you have questions about any of them, please
visit pljcommunications.com and click on the Contact tab.

101 Amazing Things About Christmas
Copyright © 2020 by PLJ Communications
Published by Harvest House Publishers
Eugene, Oregon 97408
www.harvesthousepublishers.com

ISBN 978-0-7369-7981-8 (Hardcover)
ISBN 978-0-7369-7982-5 (eBook)

Printed in China
20 21 22 23 24 25 26 27 28 /RDS/ 10 9 8 7 6 5 4 3 2 1

THE WONDER OF
Christmas

CHRISTMAS. We cherish it, worry about it, and seek its true meaning. We look back fondly on Christmases past and look forward hopefully to Christmases yet to be. We sing about it, talk about it, write about it, dream of it, and even Tweet about it.

But there's one thing we should not do: lose the wonder of Christmas. Doing so would be like failing to open the most-cherished gift under the tree. Or failing to appreciate the gift of a Savior born 2,000 years ago, God's amazing gift to us all.

This book celebrates Christmas in all its glory, foibles, humor, and mysteries. In the following pages, you'll find a veritable feast of things Christmas—the historical, the sentimental, the humorous, and the downright wonderful. This book's creators hope we will help you and those you love celebrate the many ways Christmas can surprise, delight, amaze, comfort, and enrich one's life like no other season on earth.

1
A Way, in a Manger

THE PERSON CREDITED with devising the Christmas manger scene is Saint Francis of Assisi. In 1223, Saint Francis decided he wanted to re-create the night Jesus was born. According to one of Francis's biographers (his disciple Thomas of Celano), he wanted to "make a memorial of that Child who was born in Bethlehem, and in some sort behold with bodily eyes His infant hardships; how He lay in a manger on the hay, with the ox and ass standing by."

In the small town of Greccio, located between Rome and Assisi, Francis and his friend Giovanni Vellita built a stable and dressed people as Mary, Joseph, and the shepherds. He used a wax doll to represent the baby Jesus. The animals, including a donkey, some cows, and some sheep, were all real. Saint Francis hoped his manger scene would help people remember God's gift of his Son. He summoned the town's 1,500 residents to his display, and, as people viewed the spectacle, Francis read from the Scriptures.

Today, Saint Francis's tradition carries on in small and large scales. One example of the latter takes place in the town hall of The Hague, where a life-sized nativity scene is erected, with actual people and animals, including donkeys, oxen, and camels borrowed from a nearby zoo.

2

Merry Christmas—

AND YOU'RE UNDER ATTACK!

AS THE YEAR 1776 drew to a close, the Revolutionary War seemed to be going the way of the British. The Colonial forces had lost a string of battles, and morale was low. Many men deserted the Continental Army.

General George Washington realized he needed to do something or the war was lost. On Christmas Day, the general led 2,400 troops on a dangerous nocturnal crossing of the icy Delaware River. Washington's forces successfully navigated the river and crept into New Jersey on the day after Christmas. They launched a surprise attack on Trenton, with Washington figuring that the enemy Hessian soldiers would be bloated and disoriented after indulging in too much holiday food and drink.

Washington's daring gamble paid off. The Colonial forces dominated the enemy with minimal bloodshed. Then Washington and his army reversed course and recrossed the Delaware—now with almost 1,000 Hessian prisoners in tow.

The victory energized the entire Continental Army and changed the course of the war. Washington went on to lead more successful efforts (including the battles of Assunpink Creek and Princeton) and eventually won the war.

Martin Luther:

HISTORIC REFORMER. . .
AND CHRISTMAS TREE DECORATOR?

MARTIN LUTHER, a Protestant reformer who lived about 500 years ago, is credited with inventing the custom of bringing a Christmas tree into a home and then decorating it with shiny, shimmering ornaments and tinsel.

One winter evening, Luther was strolling in the woods, admiring tall fir trees standing against a starry sky. He cut down one of the trees, carried it home, and decorated it with candles. Then he gathered his children around the twinkling candles and told them how they reminded him of the stars that shone above Bethlehem the night Jesus was born.

"THIS CHILD IS THE SAVIOR AND
FAR BETTER THAN HEAVEN AND EARTH.
HIM, THEREFORE, WE SHOULD
ACKNOWLEDGE AND ACCEPT;
CONFESS HIM AS OUR SAVIOR
IN EVERY NEED, CALL UPON HIM,
AND NEVER DOUBT THAT HE WILL SAVE US
FROM ALL MISFORTUNE. AMEN."

— MARTIN LUTHER
(from a Christmas sermon delivered on Christmas Day, 1530)

4

Noel News

THE WORD "NOEL" is seen and heard a lot during Christmastime, but many people are unaware of its origins. "Noel" is how people say "Christmas" in France. (The French version of "Merry Christmas" is *Joyeux Noël.*) According to several French sources, the word comes from shortening the French phrase *les bonnes nouvelles,* which means "the good news"—the good news of Jesus's birth in Bethlehem.

However, several dictionaries, including *Merriam-Webster,* trace noel's origins to the Latin word *natalis,* or birthday.

Incidentally, "Noel!" is more than a greeting. A noel is also a Christmas carol. Noels were being sung in Latin and French hundreds of years before the word found its way into the English language in the 1800s.

Green Is a
CHRISTMAS COLOR

LONG BEFORE CHRIST'S BIRTH, people used evergreen boughs to decorate their homes for winter. The greenery reminded everyone that plants, now dormant, would return with spring. As Christianity became popular in Europe, especially in Germany, the greenery tradition was incorporated into religious celebrations.

Christians decorated evergreen trees, representing the Garden of Eden. The trees were called Paradise Trees, a nod to the biblical Adam and Eve. The tree really became popular when Queen Victoria decorated a Christmas tree to honor her husband's German heritage. She was a trendsetter. Periodicals of the day showcased the royal Christmas trees, and by 1860, most well-off British homes had one. The tradition took a little longer to cross the pond, but by 1900, one in five American families had a Christmas tree. Today, about 30 million real Christmas trees are sold in the US annually.

6

Summer Santa in Silk?

IN BRAZIL, PAPAI NOEL (or Father Christmas), who hails from Greenland, not the North Pole, is the fellow who is traditionally credited with bringing gifts to all the children. And, because in South America December 25 occurs in the middle of summer, the Brazilian Santa eschews the heavy red suit with the fur cuffs in favor of a lighter and more breathable fabric: silk.

Father Christmas is not the only person who strives to keep it cool during the Brazilian Christmas season. Many families try to beat the holiday heat by spending Christmas at the beach. Thus, one of the most popular holiday desserts is ice cream.

"MY IDEA OF CHRISTMAS,
WHETHER OLD-FASHIONED OR MODERN,
IS VERY SIMPLE: LOVING OTHERS."

—BOB HOPE

A Story Yule Love

IF YOU'VE EVER ENJOYED the warmth of a Yule log, thank a Norseman. *Yule* is Norse for "jolly"—an appropriate adjective for the mood at Yule-time festivals of long ago. The celebration of Yule kicked off the winter solstice. The Norse used the shortest day of the year to embark on a 12-day feast, marked by the singing of carols and the burning of the Yule log. Depending on the size of the log, it might continue burning for the entire 12 days. The Norse believed that each spark from the log was a harbinger of good things to come in the new year ahead.

Today, some people saturate a log with fragrant spices and then ask children to distribute holly sprigs tied with bright ribbons to Christmas guests. The log is ignited, and once it's ablaze, everyone tosses in the holly sprigs, symbolizing the wrongs of the past that are now forgiven and forgotten in the grace-filled spirit of the holy season.

DID YOU KNOW?

Sprinkling salt on a Yule log will make its flames bright yellow.

8

Nicholas:

A REAL SAINT OF A GUY

WHILE THE EASTER BUNNY and the Tooth Fairy are inventions of the imagination, there really was a Saint Nicholas. Nicholas, widely recognized as a Christian saint, served as bishop of Myra (modern-day Turkey) in the fourth century. He was known for his good deeds, including giving gifts. He also saw various miracles credited to his intercessory prayers. Thus, he earned the moniker "Saint Nicholas the Wonderworker."

After the Reformation, Saint Nicholas was, for the most part, forgotten in Protestant Europe. However, Holland kept the legend alive for the saint, whom they called *Sinterklaas*. The Dutch told their children that Saint Nicholas would arrive on horseback on his feast day (traditionally December 6), dressed in a bishop's red robe and miter. He was said to be accompanied by Zwarte Piet, a freed slave who helped his saintly partner distribute sweets and presents to good children, and lumps of coal or potatoes to the misbehaved.

When Dutch people began to settle New Amsterdam (aka New York City) they brought this tradition with them.

In paintings, Nicholas was often depicted in a red-and-white bishop's robe. While he was never officially canonized, Nicholas is recognized as the patron saint of many cities and countries worldwide.

It's All Downhill
FROM HERE

TOTING A SLED to the local hill is a favorite Christmas tradition for those blessed with the right topography and weather.

Sleds were originally used by delivery boys in snowy areas, but in the 1870s, folks in both Europe and the United States began toying with the idea that a sled could be used for fun as well as work. Before the 1870s ended, you could find a variety of sleds advertised in your household Montgomery Ward catalog, with prices ranging from 60 cents to $1.15 for a deluxe model.

By 1915, the Flexible Flyer company was the American king of sled making with its brand of steel-bladed and steerable contraptions. During the 1915 sledding season, the Pennsylvania company sold 2,000 sleds a day. Today, an original Flexible Flyer is on display at the Smithsonian Institution, and replicas of this sledding classic are available at toy and gadget stores.

Skating Figures

LIKE ITS COUSIN SLEDDING, ice-skating began out of necessity rather than for sport or fun. The earliest ice-skaters (circa 3000 BCE) were Fins concerned with transportation, not recreation. They used skates made with sharpened horse or cow bones, which were attached to their shoes with leather straps. Skaters used a long stick (or two poles) to help power themselves along and to steer.

The Dutch were the first to use iron blades—and they are also credited with inventing the double-edged blade that allows skaters to maneuver skillfully without poles.

By the 1700s, ice-skating was a popular winter pastime in Europe, and it quickly spread to North America. Figure skating became an official Olympic sport in 1908.

Incidentally, the largest natural skating rink is the Rideau Canal Skateway in Ottawa, Canada. The canal is 4.8 miles long and occupies the space of 90 Olympic-sized skating rinks. Rideau began operations more than 50 years ago, and today it welcomes about 1.5 million skaters each year, even though it is open for only about two months each season.

Christmas

1901

HAVE YOU EVER WONDERED what Christmas was like long ago in America?

Well, if you could go back in time to the year 1901, you would find many differences from today's celebrations.

First, only 20 percent of households displayed a Christmas tree during the holidays.

As for the most popular toys, here are a few of the hot items, along with their average retail prices:

- Sled: 98¢
- Doll cradle: 10¢
- Sleeping-eye doll: 89¢
- Ice skates: 49¢ a pair

As for stocking stuffers, the hot item in 1901 was a new confection from the Hershey Chocolate Company: the Hershey bar. And the cost was a budget-friendly 1 cent per bar. (That's about 30 cents today.) If you are wondering about Hershey's Kisses, they didn't start appearing in Christmas stockings until 1907.

DID YOU KNOW?

Christmas 1977 saw *Star Wars* become so popular that toy makers struggled to meet demands. Kenner had to create 600,000 empty IOU action-figure boxes to be sold at retail.

12
Understanding
THE MISTLETOE

IF YOU'VE EVER stolen a kiss under the mistletoe, thank the Druids. The Druids believed the mistletoe plant to be a symbol of peace, vibrancy, and good health. It was so esteemed because it blossomed even during the harshest winters. Thus, the politically tenuous negotiations between warring Celtic tribes were sometimes held under branches sporting the parasitic plants. Under the mistletoe, the negotiators would lay down their arms as a sign of truce. Later, when many Celts converted to Christianity (beginning in the early part of the third century), mistletoe survived as an emblem of goodwill and friendship.

During Christmastime, mistletoe was hung over doorways, where guests were often greeted with a friendly kiss or "holy kiss"—a term from the New Testament. (See Romans 16:16.)

The custom continued to morph, and during the eighteenth century in England it became permissible for an unmarried man to kiss any unmarried woman whom he happened to catch standing beneath mistletoe. If that kiss was refused, the man in question was thought to be doomed to a lifetime of misfortune.

Incidentally, while kissing under mistletoe can be enjoyable, don't try to eat it. Both its berries and leaves are toxic, and potentially lethal, to humans and pets.

The ABCs
OF THE CHRISTMAS LETTER

OUR ANNUAL HOLIDAY CARDS or newsletters provide the chance to connect (or reconnect) with family and friends. Composing these pieces of correspondence can be daunting, but social-expression experts Angela Ensminger and Keely Chace (authors of *On a Personal Note: A Guide to Writing Notes with Style*) provide some helpful tips to help ensure that your annual Christmas missive hits the mark.

1. Be creative and try to enjoy writing!

2. Provide details—such as which kinds of decorations are showing up around town, what kind of activities are taking place, and what the weather is like.

3. Let people know what's on your mind—thinking back on years gone by or looking ahead. And let people know your hopes and warm wishes for them. A meaningful holiday correspondence reflects a theme, such as love, peace, reflection, faith, or gratitude.

4. If you face writer's block, use a prompt like "This Christmas, I'm grateful for…" or "Here's my special Christmas wish for you…"

Holy Holly?

HOLLY, WITH ITS CRIMSON BERRIES and vivid green leaves, is one of the Christmas season's most striking decorations. This plant has long been a part of various cultures' celebrations. In ancient times, it was thought to be magical because of its unusually shiny leaves and ability to bear fruit in winter. Additionally, some religious poems and songs portray holly berries as a symbol of Christ and his death on the cross.

For some, the red berries represent the blood Jesus shed on the cross when he was crucified. (One ancient legend suggests that the berries were originally white but became red after the crucifixion.) Additionally, the plant's pointed leaves symbolize the crown of thorns placed on Jesus's head. In German, holly is known as *christdorn* or "Christ thorn."

However, holly is best enjoyed by the eyes, not the tongue. Holly berries, while eaten by some birds and wild animals, are mildly toxic to humans and household pets. The berries can cause vomiting and diarrhea, two things that will not enhance one's holiday celebration.

15

Poinsettia Pointers

EVER WONDER WHY the hard-to-spell poinsettia plant has become so closely tied to Christmas? The legend began long ago in Mexico, where it was traditional to leave gifts for Jesus on a church altar on Christmas Eve.

As the legend goes, a poor boy was sad because he had no gift to leave for the Savior. Upset by his poverty, the boy knelt outside a church window and prayed. In the spot where he knelt, a beautiful plant sprouted: a plant with vibrant red leaves. In Mexico, this plant is called the "Flower of the Holy Night."

The first US minister to Mexico was Joel Roberts Poinsett (appointed to his post in 1825). He was so impressed by the Flower of the Holy Night's beauty that he brought samples back to the United States (in 1828), where the flower was renamed "poinsettia" in his honor.

16

Have Yourself
A MERRY MEDIEVAL CHRISTMAS

IF YOU GREW UP in medieval England, what would your Christmas dinner look like? If you were wealthy and/or famous, you could enjoy a main course of peacock or swan.

If you were a bit less fortunate…how does boar's head sound?

In the 1700s, turkey and beef started to replace boar, to the relief of taste buds across the country.

And what would a holiday meal be without Christmas pudding—which was a porridge known as frumenty (a fancy word for wheat or corn boiled in milk).

As cooks experimented, dried plums, eggs, and bits of meat were added for flavor. Because of the plums, frumenty was often called plum pudding.

One doesn't typically attach spiritual significance to pudding, but some families insisted that their pudding be crafted with 13 ingredients, symbolizing Jesus and the 12 disciples. And others invited every family member to take turns stirring the pudding, from east to west, in honor of the Magi.

In 1664, the Puritans banned Christmas pudding, citing it as "bad custom." The ban remained in place for 50 years. Then, in 1714, King George I reestablished the dish as part of the Christmas meal. Not for any theological or philosophical reasons. He just really liked pudding.

Your Gift

IS IN THE CARDS

BECAUSE EVERY CHRISTMAS GIFT LIST contains at least one person who is hard to buy for, gift cards have become big business for the holidays. According to Hallmark, consumers purchase an average of four gift cards per year, with a total cash value of $156.

"Gift cards are popular," says retail expert Mary Nacrelli (who has worked for Hallmark and Blue Cross & Blue Shield), "because they are convenient and flexible. Shoppers can wait until the last minute to purchase a gift, because gift cards are always in stock."

She adds, "The stigma of giving a gift card is long gone; people love receiving them—it's the gift of shopping."

Despite the growth of e-gift cards, traditional plastic gift cards are still the most popular choice, preferred by 75 percent of buyers. This preference mirrors (somewhat) the revenue generated by both types. E-gift cards represent approximately $18 billion of the $130 billion total market.

Which cards are most popular? Here are the top 5, according to Giftcards.com:

1. restaurant
2. Visa/MasterCard/American Express prepaid cards
3. department store
4. coffee shop
5. specialty clothing/shoes/apparel

Free Trees

FOR THE PRESIDENT!

BEING PRESIDENT of the United States comes with a lot of fringe benefits, one of which is a free Christmas tree. The National Christmas Tree Association has given a Christmas tree to every US President and his family since Lyndon B. Johnson.

According to some sources, Franklin Pierce, the fourteenth president of the United States, was the first to display a Christmas tree in the White House (in 1856). However, the White House Historical Association lists Benjamin Harrison as the true Christmas tree pioneer. According to the association, in 1889, Harrison placed the tree in the second floor oval room and decorated it with candles, toys, and various ornaments designed to dazzle the Harrison grandchildren.

Electricity was installed in the White House in 1891, and in 1894, Grover Cleveland ordered up a tree decorated with red, white, and blue electric bulbs, delighting his young daughters.

Theodore Roosevelt, a staunch conservationist, refused to have a tree cut down even to decorate the White House. However, this didn't mean he was a grinch. In 1903, for example, the president and first lady Edith Roosevelt hosted a "Christmas carnival" for more than 500 children. The event featured dinner, dancing, music, gifts, and an ice-cream dessert shaped like Santa Claus.

19

Letters to Santa
(IN INDIANA)

MANY CHILDREN leave a note or letter for Santa by the family fireplace, along with the Big Guy's milk and cookies. Others, however, prefer a more official route.

Santa Claus, Indiana, has a population of only 2,000 people, but it receives many, many times that number of letters each holiday season because of a tradition that dates to the 1920s. For decades, every letter received in time for Christmas (usually by December 20) receives a response, and the program is free (although donations are welcome).

If you know a child who wants to send an official piece of correspondence to the Indiana town, the US Postal Service requests that he or she follows these guidelines:

1. Letters should be addressed to:
    Santa Claus, P.O. Box 1, Santa Claus, IN 47579.

2. The sender's city, state, and ZIP code should be included.

3. Children should ask an adult to help them spell everything correctly.

4. Letters only, please. (No candy, cookies, or hay for the reindeer should be enclosed.)

For more information, visit santaclausind.org.

20

Wreaths and the
WELL-ROUNDED CHRISTMAS

HAVE YOU EVER WONDERED why evergreen trees and wreaths are so closely linked to Christmas and the Advent season? It's no accident.

Evergreen trees were truly inspiring to the people of northern Europe. Because they endured long, harsh winters marked by cold, dark nights and brutally short days, the climate-defying strength and grandeur of evergreens were awe inspiring. Here were trees not even winter could defeat. Because of the trees' strength in the face of impossible odds, Christians saw them as a symbol for their faith.

During the Advent season, they took limbs from evergreen trees and fashioned them into wheel-shaped decorations. During the early part of the Middle Ages, they began placing a candle in the wreath to symbolize the light Jesus brought into the world with his birth. These Advent wreaths were the first symbols to enjoy widespread use among Christians of the North.

At first, people made marks on the candle to represent each day of Advent. Later (in the mid-800s), believers began using more candles, with a new one being lit during each day of Advent.

"EVERY YEAR WE CELEBRATE
THE HOLY SEASON OF ADVENT, O GOD."

— KARL RAHNER

21

The Christmas Card

PIONEERS

ACCORDING TO Hallmark Cards, Inc., Christmas is the biggest card-sending holiday in the United States, as people send about 2.2 billion cards each season. (Another half a million e-cards are sent as well.) People send cards for many reasons, but most do so because they know how good it feels when *they* receive a holiday greeting, and they want others to enjoy the same feeling. Christmas is, by far, *the* season for greeting cards.

Who sent the first Christmas cards? There is a bit of debate on this one, but most historians agree that an Englishman named John Horsley is the pioneer. In 1843, he printed a card design for his friend Sir Henry Cole, a designer and the founder of the Victoria and Albert Museum. (Horsley was a painter and a Royal Academician.)

That card (printed on cardboard) showed people feeding and clothing the poor in one scene, while another pictured a family Christmas party with everyone drinking wine—including a child. This made the card somewhat controversial, but it sold well. The words were simple: "Merry Christmas and a happy New Year to you."

Of the original 1,000 cards Horsley printed for Cole, only 12 are known to exist today. At auction, one of those rare cards sold for $35,800 in 2001.

The Horsley cards were hand colored and sold for one shilling, a relatively high price for the day. (One shilling in 1843 equals about $9.60 in today's US dollars.)

Horsley's creation cost one pence (or penny) to mail, while the card itself was a shilling (as we have just learned). One shilling is the equivalent of 12 pence. Imagine if today's most popular greeting card was 12 times the price of the stamp to mail it. (At current stamp prices, that means a greeting card price of $6.60.)

Louis Prang, a Polish-born lithographer and designer, is credited with introducing Christmas cards to the United States, circa 1875. Prang's first cards featured simple floral designs adapted from some business cards he created. After that, Christmas cards changed with the times. They became patriotic during times of war and began to carry religious words and imagery in the 1950s. Today, the annual awards for excellence in greeting cards are called the Louis Awards in Prang's honor. In addition to being a greeting card pioneer, Prang was also an advocate of art education. He published a variety of books and tools for budding artists and designers. By the 1870s, he was publishing art education texts for public schools as well as art schools and institutes. And by 1881, he was printing more than 5 million Christmas cards a year.

Merry Christmas,
FROM YOUR KING

FOR PEOPLE in the United Kingdom, the annual Christmas message is one of the highlights of the holiday season. This tradition was started by King George V (grandfather of Queen Elizabeth II) in 1932 as part of an effort to call attention to the newly created Empire Service, now better known as the BBC World Service.

The 1932 speech, which the king developed with famed writer and poet Rudyard Kipling, was broadcast live over the wireless from a small office at Sandringham.

The tradition continues today, although people can now experience the message from a variety of sources. In 2012, for example, Queen Elizabeth's message was broadcast via 3D television for the first time.

Here is King George's 1932 message in its entirety:

Through one of the marvels of modern science, I am enabled, this Christmas Day, to speak to all my peoples throughout the Empire. I take it as a good omen that wireless should have reached its present perfection at a time when the Empire has been linked in closer union. For it offers us immense possibilities to make that union closer still.

It may be that our future may lay upon us more than one stern test. Our past will have taught us how to meet it unshaken. For the present, the works to which we are all equally bound is to arrive at a reasoned tranquility within our borders; to regain prosperity without self-seeking; and to carry with us those whom the burden of past years has disheartened or overborne.

My life's aim has been to serve as I might, toward those ends. Your loyalty, your confidence in me, has been my abundant reward.

I speak now from my home and from my heart to you all. To men and women so cut off by the snows, the desert, or the sea, that only voices out of the air can reach them; to those cut off from fuller life by blindness, sickness, or infirmity; and to those who are celebrating this day with their children and grandchildren.

To all—to each—I wish a Happy Christmas. God Bless You!

23

I'm Dreaming
OF A WHITE (HOUSE) CHRISTMAS

MODERN CHRISTMAS CELEBRATIONS in the White House are grand affairs, as you have probably seen on TV and in social media over the past few years.

In the early 1800s, however, the White House Christmas celebration was not a big deal. The first family would decorate the White House with simple wreaths, garlands, and various ornaments. The celebrations were typically quiet. (Christmas was not declared an official federal holiday until June 26, 1870, during the presidency of Ulysses S. Grant.)

The first official White House party was held in 1800. President John Adams and first lady Abigail Adams made their four-year-old granddaughter, Susanna Boylston Adams, the special guest. (Young Susanna lived with her grandparents at the time.) Various government officials attended, bringing their families with them. (It's worth noting that President Adams was the first resident of the famous building. He and Abigail moved in to the residence in 1800, even though construction was not complete.)

In 1835, Andrew Jackson made Christmas a frolic for the children of his household. The Jacksonian holiday celebration included games, dancing, and a multicourse dinner. The climax was an indoor snowball fight. No actual snowballs were used. Instead, Jackson provided White House—safe balls, made from cotton.

When Christmas
GETS YOUR GOAT

MOST AMERICANS don't associate a goat with Christmas unless it's one of the background animals in a manger scene. But in Sweden, one of the most unique holiday traditions is the Yule Goat. Usually made of straw, this goat has one mission: to guard the Christmas tree.

Why straw? Straw is commonly used as a holiday decoration in Scandinavian homes because it reminds people that Jesus was born in a humble manger, with straw as his bed.

And no Christmas goat is like the one in the Swedish city of Gävle. Ever since 1966, the community has joined forces to build a 43-foot-high goat to officially kick off the Advent season.

Sadly, a parallel tradition has also emerged. For more than 50 years, a group of pranksters has routinely set fire to the goat. Efforts are faithfully launched to save the goat, but since the late 1960s, it has survived through Christmas only a dozen times.

Advent-ures

THE 24 DAYS BEFORE CHRISTMAS are called Advent. The Advent season begins on the fourth Sunday before Christmas and ends on Christmas Eve. During Advent, people around the world remember and celebrate Jesus's birth in Bethlehem. They ponder what that birth meant to those who lived long ago—and what it means to people around the world today.

Many churches and families commemorate the Advent season by the lighting of Advent candles, following an Advent calendar, or reading a series of biblical or devotional passages.

Advent has been celebrated since at least the fourth century. Originally, Advent marked a time to prepare for Christmas, and for the second coming of Jesus Christ. Today, many people view it as a countdown to Christmas.

The Advent calendar, with surprises or treats behind little doors or flaps, is credited to Gerhard Lang in the early 1900s. Lang was inspired by a calendar his mother made for him when he was a child. It featured 24 colored pictures attached to a large piece of cardboard.

Today, Advent calendars contain everything from candy to LEGO bricks. Several years ago, one company even produced a Noah's Ark Advent Calendar. Though it was historically dubious, the calendar went on to be a big seller.

Hogmanay
TRUMPS CHRISTMAS?

PEOPLE IN THE UNITED STATES sometimes wonder if Christmas is as popular elsewhere in the world.

The answer? It depends. For example, Scotland has historically given prominence to Hogmanay (or New Year's Eve), rather than Christmas.

But it's not because the Scots don't like Christmas. There is a simple reason they don't celebrate Christmas in a big way. For a long time it was illegal to do so.

In the mid-1600s, Scottish Parliament banned Christmas, and that ban stood for more than 300 years. (Christmas was officially made legal again in 1958.)

As with other Christmas bans throughout history, the attack on the holiday came from within the church rather than from without. John Knox, a leader of the Scottish Reformation and the founder of the Presbyterian Church of Scotland, led the ban. He believed Christians should celebrate only holidays specifically mentioned in the Bible.

So celebrating Christmas was strongly discouraged, starting in the late 1500s, which were also the latter years of Knox's life and ministry. Knox's view of Christmas continued to influence people even after his death, and the holiday was officially prohibited by law in 1640.

Caring, Sharing, Caroling

THE CUSTOM of traveling carolers goes all the way back to the Middle Ages, when Nativity plays were popular. In Slovakia, some innovative performers decided to take their show on the road, so to speak. They carried a small home-made Nativity scene (made of carved wood and painted paper) from cottage to cottage to sing of Jesus's birth for their neighbors. On particularly inclement nights, the brave carolers were welcomed into the cottages, where they could warm themselves before pressing on.

In the mid-1800s in Victorian England, the tradition continued. Neighbors who visited one another to wish God's blessings and good cheer incorporated songs into their visits. In Victorian England, caroling was popular not only on Christmas, but on other holidays, like May Day.

The tradition has spread and expanded since then. In today's United Kingdom, for example, carolers raise their voices—and raise money for charity at the same time. Carol services are also popular in the UK. One of the most famous carol services, dubbed the Festival of Nine Lessons and Carols, is held in the chapel of King's College in Cambridge. It has become so popular that it's broadcast on television, radio, and the internet for the people who can't be there in person.

28

This Christmas,

DON'T HOG THE NOG

WHAT IS IT ABOUT the holidays that inspires people to drink a beverage containing raw eggs? No one knows for sure, but many historians agree that today's eggnog is probably inspired by a medieval drink called "posset" (which first gained popularity during the late 1500s in England). Posset was a concoction of eggs, milk, figs, sugar, and sherry. In such times, the ingredients were expensive, so posset (or, later, eggnog) was usually a beverage of the rich.

While it was primarily a dessert beverage, posset was also thought to be a curative for colds and fevers. *The Journals of the House of Lords* reports that in 1620, King Charles I was prescribed posset by his personal physician. Posset was traditionally served warm from cups shaped like teapots. Shakespeare mentions the beverage several times in his writings, including *Hamlet*.

The nog became a holiday drink when the colonists brought it over from England. To economize, they had to forego the figs, and they substituted rum for sherry. The first eggnog produced in the United States was created in Captain John Smith's 1607 Jamestown settlement.

Why the nog moniker? It's unclear, but nog might be short for noggin, which was a wooden cup.

Santa vs. the Colonel?

IF YOU EVER SPEND CHRISTMAS in Japan, forget about the turkey, ham, or stuffing. Chicken is the entrée of choice. Specifically, chicken that is fried Kentucky-style. Even though the country's Christian population is only about 1.5 million (or 1 percent of the total), Christmas Day finds thousands of families flocking to KFC. The demand has become so great that reservations are often required. Savvy celebrators make those reservations weeks in advance.

The trend started in 1947 when the Colonel and company launched a "Kentucky for Christmas!" campaign, which was first aimed at tourists and expats. The dinner featured fried chicken and wine, something that resembled (at least somewhat) Christmas meals in the West. The 1947 effort was so successful that the promotion became an annual event. By the 1970s, Kentucky Fried Chicken and Christmas were as strongly linked as mashed potatoes and gravy. Tourists and expats began encountering Japanese Christians at the fast-food chain's restaurants.

Today, KFC is the traditional Christmas feast in the Land of the Rising Sun.

The Recipe

FOR HUMBLE PIE

WHAT IS YOUR FAVORITE kind of holiday pie? Pumpkin? Pecan? Cherry? French Silk? How about humble pie? To most of us, it's a metaphor. When we see someone acting prideful, we observe, "That person needs to eat some humble pie!"

But humble pie was not symbolic hundreds of years ago. In medieval times, the well-off families in Europe dined on goose at Christmastime, or perhaps venison. When the Americas were discovered in the fifteenth century, turkey found its way onto holiday menus.

For poor families, however, fine cuts of meat were out of the question. They often couldn't afford venison, goose, or turkey, and, even when they could, in some cases they weren't allowed to eat the choice cuts. However, sometimes a lord or other aristocrat would be inspired by the Christmas spirit and would donate the less-desired (or unwanted) parts of a deer or other animal to his servants or other less-fortunate families. These discards were known as "offal" or the "umbles."

To make these umbles go as far as possible, they were mixed with other ingredients, such as potatoes and assorted leftovers, and tossed into a pie crust. Thus, "We're having umble pie this Christmas" became a common refrain.

Not to Mince Words...

HAVE YOU EVER enjoyed mince pie (or mincemeat pie) at Christmastime? This traditional dish has rich religious significance. In Tudor times (1485–1603), mince pies were baked from 13 ingredients, representing Jesus and his 12 disciples. Mutton was often included because it represented the shepherds who heard the news of Jesus's birth—and the fact that Jesus is the Good Shepherd. The spices (such as cinnamon, cloves, and nutmeg) symbolized the gifts presented to Jesus by the wise men.

And, just in case people needed more symbolism in their meal, mince pies were originally baked in rectangular shapes, representing the infant Jesus's manger crib. The pies were small (rather like today's hand pies), and it was believed to bring blessings if one were to eat a pie a day for the 12 days of Christmas.

A Pet-Friendly
CHRISTMAS

PET OWNERS love to include their cats, dogs, and other animals in their holiday celebrations. In one poll, the SPCA discovered that 73 percent of pet owners display a stocking for their pets, and 51 percent include pets in the holiday meal.

It's great to make pets a part of Christmas, but savvy pet owners know that a lot of the food served at holiday time is not safe for dogs, cats, and other critters. According to the SPCA, pet owners should keep these ten things in mind:

1. Fruitcakes and Christmas puddings can contain raisins, which can be deadly to cats and dogs due to dehydration and kidney failure.

2. Alcohol and caffeine are toxic to most pets.

3. Avocadoes contain persin, which causes a variety of symptoms, from vomiting to diarrhea to cardiac arrest. Birds are particularly sensitive to persin, but it's best to avoid feeding avocado to any pet.

4. Macadamia nuts can make a dog very sick. Symptoms include vomiting, weakness, and tremors.

5. Onions and chives contain disulfides and sulfoxides, which can harm red blood cells.

6. Peaches, plums, persimmons, and apple pips contain a substance that is a precursor of cyanide.

7. Xylitol, a common ingredient in sugarless desserts, candy, and gum can cause hypoglycemia in dogs, who seem particularly fond of sugarless gum. (The sweetener's effect on cats and other pets has not been studied, but chances are it's not good for them either.)

8. Sweet corn corncobs can cause blockages in the small intestine, sometimes requiring surgery. Don't let your dog eat corncobs or use them as a chew toy.

9. Turkey skin, pork crackling, sausages, and other fatty meats add lots of extra calories to a pet's diet, and they can lead to intense intestinal pain, vomiting, and bloody diarrhea due to pancreatitis.

10. Chocolate contains methylxanthines. When ingested by pets, these substances create a barrage of symptoms, including abnormal heart rhythms, seizures, tremors, excessive thirst, hyperactivity, and even death. To your pet, dark chocolate is the most dangerous, followed by milk chocolate and white chocolate. And be aware that baked goods can be as dangerous to your pet as candy. Baking chocolate has the highest methylxanthine content of them all.

Check with your veterinarian for specific guidelines for your pet or pets.

Christmas at Denny's

MANY AMERICANS find that planning, preparing, and hosting a Christmas Day meal is too much of a challenge. Christmas can be stressful enough without worrying if the turkey is overcooked or if one of the cousins will suffer a surprise attack from a food allergy.

That is why many people have made "Christmas at Denny's" a holiday tradition, beginning in 1953, when the first restaurants opened.

For the past several years, Christmas has been the 24/7 chain's busiest day of the year, serving almost 1.2 million guests each season.

Denny's has evolved with the times, now offering an online and mobile-ordering platform called "Denny's on Demand," which allows Christmas guests the option of a take-out or delivered meal.

Back in 1988, Denny's decided to break with tradition and give its 60,000 employees a special gift: a paid Christmas Day off for the first time in its (then) 35-year history. But there were two problems.

First, because its restaurants were always open, 700 of the 1,221 operating Denny's locations didn't have locks on the doors. And those restaurants that did have locking doors? No one knew where the keys were.

So, to make Christmas 1988 happen, management had to install locks on more than half of their buildings.

A Feast Fit for a King

WHAT IS THE LARGEST Christmas dinner you have either attended or hosted? If you have been a part of a large-scale Christmas meal, you are continuing a tradition that's more than 800 years old. By the time King John was ruling in England (from 1199 to 1216), Christmas meals were a major event.

On Christmas Day 1213, the king's guests must have arrived especially hungry and thirsty. They celebrated Christ's birth by consuming 27 hogsheads of wine (one hogshead was about 55 gallons), 400 head of pork, 3,000 fowl, 15,000 herrings, 10,000 eels, and 100 pounds of almonds. And then there were the 66 pounds of pepper used to spice up various dishes.

From that point, things got even bigger (if not necessarily better). The recipe for a Christmas pie from 1349 calls for copious amounts of pheasant, hare, capon, partridge, pigeon, rabbit, and a variety of hearts, kidneys, livers, and meatballs. The pie was spiced with pickled mushrooms and baked in a huge bird-shaped pie shell, which included a tail decorated with real bird feathers.

Christmas Cookies:
A BRIEF HISTORY

WHAT IS A HOLIDAY CELEBRATION without a Christmas cookie? (Or two, or three?)

The idea of holiday sweet treats dates to winter solstice festivals of old, from Rome to Norway to West Africa to Ireland. Groups of people gathered to celebrate the changing of the seasons, and food was a centerpiece. Celebrants feasted, knowing that a harsh winter might lie ahead. Also, because of the colder weather, animals could be slaughtered and kept safely chilled.

What's more, various fermented beverages, such as beer and wine that had been brewing since spring, were now ready to enjoy. And what would a holiday meal be without something sweet? The ancient Romans, for example, loved to take bread crusts, soak them in milk, and then fry them in oil. The crusts were then drizzled with honey before serving.

By the Middle Ages, holiday celebrations had become more religious, but celebrants still loved their food. The main dishes stayed much the same: roasted meats and wine. However, the pastry world had evolved beyond the days of fried bread with honey. Spices such as nutmeg, cinnamon, and black pepper were becoming popular, as were dried fruits such as apricots, citrons, raisins, and dates.

Cooks began to experiment, and they found that cookies made a great alternative to more expensive and labor-intensive desserts such as cakes and pies. And, unlike cakes and pies, cookies were relatively easy to transport to Christmas meals and share with family and friends.

Cookies have come a long way since the medieval days, but today's Christmas cookies share much in common with their predecessors. Cookies flavored with cinnamon, nutmeg, and ginger are still popular. In fact, today's classic gingerbread cookies would feel right at home on a medieval dessert tray. These cookies are usually sweetened with molasses rather than sugar, just as they were hundreds of years ago. (Sugar was around, of course, but it was very expensive.)

There is one key difference. There were no gingerbread men in medieval times. Queen Elizabeth I, who ruled from the mid-1500s to the early 1600s, is credited with giving gingerbread cookies that "human touch." She asked her chefs to mold cookies into the shapes of her favorite courtiers, and a new (and tasty) tradition was born.

The Case of Martin
AND THE MANGER SONG

ALMOST EVERYONE knows at least the first verse of the classic carol "Away in a Manger." And almost everyone *thinks* he or she knows the song's author: Martin Luther, the German priest who ignited the Protestant Reformation.

But, while Luther was a songwriter as well as a reformer (he wrote "A Mighty Fortress Is Our God"), the idea that he wrote "Away in a Manger" is mighty wrong.

The first two verses of the carol appeared (with no authorial attribution) in a collection titled *Little Children's Book for Schools and Families*, published in 1885. The third verse, sometimes attributed to a John T. McFarland and sometimes to "Unknown," appeared in another collection, titled *Gabriel's Vineyard Songs*, published in 1892.

Luther's name was first attached to the carol upon the publication of the 1887 songbook *Dainty Songs for Little Lads and Lasses, for Use in the Kindergarten, School, and Home*. This collection was edited by James R. Murray, who credited himself for the music and attributed the lyrics to Luther. He called the song "Luther's Cradle Hymn" and claimed that the reformer wrote the song for his children more than 400 years previously, and that it was still sung "by German mothers to their little ones."

Murray offered no proof for his claim, and it's unclear if he truly believed that Luther wrote the words or if he was using the name for publicity. Whatever the case, "Away in a Manger" became more popular than ever, and for the next 60 years, people assumed that Luther was indeed the author.

Then, in 1945, a researcher from the Library of Congress discovered that the lyrics of the first two verses came from an anonymous children's poem published in America, not Germany. Further, the poem was published in 1883, not the 1400s when Luther lived.

Today, those "author unknown" lyrics have been performed and recorded to more than 40 different musical arrangements. One of the most popular musical settings was created by William J. Kirkpatrick, whose name you might know if your church favors traditional hymns. Kirkpatrick wrote the music for such classics as "'Tis So Sweet to Trust in Jesus" and "We Have Heard the Joyful Sound."

Did Coke Invent Santa

OR JUST TURN HIM RED?

TO SOME CYNICS, Santa Claus is nothing more than an advertising tool. They believe that Coca-Cola invented Santa to sell more of its beverages. After all, Santa has been appearing in Coke ads since the 1930s, looking much like the big, jolly character we picture today when someone says "Santa."

The rumor has become so prevalent that the folks at Coca-Cola have addressed it on their website. They note, "Before Coca-Cola was invented, Santa Claus (St. Nick) had appeared in numerous illustrations and books wearing a scarlet coat. He was portrayed in a variety of ways. He could be tall and gaunt or short and elfin, sometimes distinguished and intellectual, other times rather frightening." Thus, the beverage maker didn't invent Santa, but, as they note, "Coca-Cola helped shape the image of Santa."

So, though Coke has a long relationship with Santa, the character we know today was envisioned by Thomas Nast, an American cartoonist famous for his Harper's Weekly illustrations, which graced the publication from 1863 through the early 1880s. Nast, in turn, was inspired by the famous Clement C. Moore poem "Account of a Visit from St. Nicholas."

Real News
ABOUT FAKE TREES

DO YOU DISPLAY a real tree at Christmas? Or do you put up an artificial tree that has been in the family for years and years? Both options have their advantages. However, a once-popular artificial tree quickly fell from favor at the hands of a cartoon.

Aluminum trees first showed up in 1958, and they quickly became a popular choice. They were sturdy and relatively light, and they eliminated the mess of tree sap and shedding needles. And they were shiny, with catchy names like Evergleam.

For a while, it looked as if aluminum trees were the present and the future of Christmas. Then along came Charlie Brown. *A Charlie Brown Christmas* aired for the first time in 1965. At a key point in the story, Charlie refuses to get a fake tree (defying advice from Lucy) and embarks on a search for a real one.

As the special aired in successive years, public opinion began to sway. People wanted real trees, just like the beloved Charles M. Schulz character. The artificial ones, people opined, symbolized what was wrong with Christmas. Aluminum trees were all but phased out by 1969, just four years after the first airing of the special.

39

This Christmas,
HOLD YOUR HOAXES

WITH PHRASES LIKE "the war on Christmas" floating around, it's not surprising that news of this war's battles can spread quickly, especially on social media.

A few years ago, the National Report (nationalreport.net) posted an article about Timothy Dawson, a 9-year-old San Francisco boy being suspended from school (Anon Elementary School) for greeting his teacher with the words "Merry Christmas." The story described Timothy being removed from the school cafeteria, where he was eating with friends, and hauled to the principal's office. There, he was scolded for wishing his homeroom teacher "Merry Christmas"—and given a week-long suspension.

The article went on to note that the teacher in question was an atheist who was offended by a student's display of Christmas spirit.

It didn't take long for the article to go viral, and many were incensed by the boy's treatment. There were demands that the teacher and the principal be punished for their actions.

Savvy readers, however, considered the source. They investigated the National Report website, where they found the following disclaimer:

National Report is a news and political satire web publication, which may or may not use real names, often in semi-real or mostly fictitious ways. All news articles contained within National Report are fiction...Any resemblance to the truth is purely coincidental.

If that disclaimer were not enough, one could look to other stories published on the site, including the one titled "IRS Plans to Target Leprechauns Next."

So if you hear about various anti-Christmas rumors spreading, especially on social media, and you think, *That's unbelievable*, you are probably correct.

40

A Song by a Saint?

SAINT BONAVENTURE (1221–1274) has many claims to fame. As a child, he became gravely ill but regained his health after intercessory prayer by Saint Francis of Assisi. He began university training at age 14 and went on to become a revered writer and teacher. He wrote Bible commentaries as well as ambitious works that synthesized the ideas of great theologians like Saint Augustine and classic philosophers like Aristotle.

Bonaventure (who was born Giovanni Di Fidanza) is also credited with composing the carol "Adeste Fideles" ("O Come All Ye Faithful"). But the song is not an ancient carol. It wasn't written until almost 500 years after Bonaventure's death.

The lyrics for this carol, originally penned in Latin, date to 1750. They were written by John Francis Wade, a priest, musician, and calligrapher. He was also a scholar of the musical form plainchant, which is similar to the Gregorian chant. (Historians have found seven hand-written transcripts of the song, each signed by Wade. Wade loved to send copies of his songs, embellished with calligraphy and illustrations, to churches throughout Europe in hopes they would appreciate the music and the message as much as he did.)

Today, people are still moved and inspired by the song, which is one of the few traditional carols to hit the pop music charts. It has made the top ten three different times and is regarded by some music aficionados as the greatest Christmas carol of them all. Artists who have recorded "O Come All Ye Faithful" include Mahalia Jackson, Amy Grant, Steven Curtis Chapman, Pentatonix, and Third Day.

O come, all ye faithful, joyful and triumphant!
O come ye, O come ye to Bethlehem;
Come and behold Him, born the King of Angels!

O come, let us adore Him,
O come, let us adore Him,
O come, let us adore Him, Christ the Lord.

DID YOU KNOW?

The term "carol" was originally the name of a dance, not a type of song. Eventually, the songs that accompanied the carol/dance began to be called carols too. What's more, the early carol/songs were not Christmas themed. They explored a variety of subjects, from love to mortality to the Holy Trinity.

Will the Real Santa

PLEASE STAND?

SAINT NICHOLAS. Father Christmas. Kris Kringle. Santa Claus. Are these different names for the same person, or is something else going on here? Let's try to sort things out.

Saint Nicholas was Bishop of Myra in what is now Turkey. Nicholas devoted his life to caring for the poor. His parents died when he was young, and he used his inheritance to help the less fortunate. He was known to deliver gifts of gold or money secretly to people in need, including dropping it down a chimney.

Nicholas was also known as a confessor, someone who publicly confessed Christ during times of persecution, who remained faithful despite any imprisonment, torture, or exile.

He died on December 6, 343, and was eventually declared a saint. That's why December 6 is Saint Nicholas Day. (There is no official date for his canonization, but historical records indicate that churches were being named after him as early as the 500s.)

Various cultures celebrated Saint Nicholas Day by inviting children to place their stockings or shoes in a conspicuous place so that "Saint Nick" could fill them with gifts of fruit, nuts, and candy.

Eventually, the legend of Saint Nick made it to North America, where the saint became known as *Sinterklaas*, the name of a festival celebrated in the Netherlands and Belgium. (In Dutch culture, Saint Nicholas and *Sinterklaas* are distinct people, but their legends became mixed.)

In America, for example, Saint Nick and *Sinterklaas* morphed into Santa Claus, and the custom of hanging stockings jumped from December 6 to Christmas.

The legend grew with the publication of the Clement C. Moore poem "Account of a Visit from St. Nicholas," although the character is described as an "elf," not a saint. A few decades later (in 1881), cartoonist Thomas Nast rendered Santa Claus wearing a red suit with white fur trim.

Meanwhile, in parts of Europe, people were losing interest in the Nicholas legend, but they still loved the idea of giving and receiving gifts, especially surprise gifts. So Saint Nick morphed into "Father Christmas." Father Christmas was not a reverent bishop. He was a partier who enjoyed raucous celebrations.

What about Kris Kringle? We have Protestant Reformer Martin Luther to thank for that permutation. In the 1500s, Luther was troubled by the growing legend of Saint Nick. He thought that it was against Scripture to revere saints or to pray to them. So he and some of his followers introduced the *Christkind* (German for Christ Child). Luther claimed that *Christkind*, not Saint Nick, would visit homes on Christmas Eve to provide presents for the children.

As the years, passed, Christkind transformed into Kris Kringle. In the 1840s, people in the United States were using Kris Kringle and Santa Claus interchangeably.

By the early twentieth century, Santa Claus became *the* go-to moniker.

A Christmas Legend

ONE OF THE MOST POPULAR Christmas legends concerns a young Inuit boy who listened carefully as one of his teachers explained why people give gifts at Christmastime—to continue the tradition of love and generosity displayed at the first Christmas.

When December 25 arrived, the boy brought his teacher a piece of weather-polished whale bone.

"Where did you find such a beautiful item?" the teacher asked.

The youth named the spot several miles away across the frozen landscape. The teacher was touched. "This is beautiful, but you didn't need to trek so far to get a gift for me."

The boy smiled. "The long walk is part of the gift."

At Christmastime, and always, it truly is the thought that counts.

43

Reginald the

RED-NOSED REINDEER?

WHILE THE POPULARITY of reindeer as the engine for Santa's sleigh is largely due to Clement C. Moore's "The Night Before Christmas," Moore wasn't the first to pair Santa with hoofed partners. Long before the publication of Moore's signature work, Russian folklore depicted "Father Frost" arriving in villages in a reindeer-drawn sleigh.

Similarly, the Norse held that the mythical god Odin rode his eight-legged steed Sleipnir through the air to make sure that people were behaving. In Holland, incidentally, Saint Nicholas is said to ride Sleipnir even today.

By the way, did you know that the most famous reindeer, Rudolph, wasn't part of Moore's team? Young Rudolph didn't come along until the 1939 publication of a Montgomery Ward promotional coloring book created by Robert L. May. May considered the names Reginald and Rollo before settling on Rudolph. (In its first year of publication, Montgomery Ward distributed 2.4 million copies of *Rudolph the Red-Nosed Reindeer*.)

However, it wasn't the story that made Rudolph a household name; it was the 1949 release of the Gene Autry single "Rudolph the Red-Nosed Reindeer." (The lyrics to the song were penned by Johnny Marks, Robert L. May's brother-in-law.)

Reindeer Roll Call

EVER WONDER about the *official* roll call order of Santa's most famous reindeer? Here it is, straight from the pen of Clement C. Moore in the poem "Account of a Visit from St. Nicholas," first published in New York's *Troy Sentinel* on December 23, 1823:

| Dasher | Dancer | Prancer | Vixen |
| Comet | Cupid | Dunder | Blixem |

If those last two names tripped you up, you are not alone. It's supposed to be "Donner" and "Blixen," right?

Well, yes and no. When Moore was assigning names to his reindeer, he took two monikers from the Dutch exclamation, "Dunder and Blixem!" (Thunder and lightning, respectively.)

However, in 1837, publisher Charles Fenno Hoffman printed a version of "A Visit from Saint Nicholas" that included several variations on the original. Blixem became Blixen (so that it would rhyme with Vixen), and Dunder became Donder, which brought the spelling of the name in line with the way most English folks pronounced it.

Why did Donder become "Donner"? Some think Gene Autry made that change when he recorded "Rudolph the Red-Nosed Reindeer" in 1949. However, "Donner" appeared in several printed sources well before 1949. (Some references date to the early 1900s.)

So, perhaps Donner will remain a Christmas mystery.

You've Reached

THE PHONE OF SANTA...MAYBE

PERHAPS THE NEXT BEST THING to meeting Santa Claus at the mall or elsewhere is calling him on the phone. It's no surprise, then, that several "Real Santa" hotlines have been promoted via social media during the past several Christmas seasons. The results have been mixed—and mixed up.

Parents and other adults who want to connect kids with Santa should do their research—and beware of any promotions or rumors they encounter on social media. Find a program you know is legitimate and safe. Ask people you can trust. Research possible scams. One place to start is the website FreeConferenceCall.com, which offers its own Santa hotline, established in 2009. The site also provides information on other reputable options.

But even after doing all the homework, an adult should call the number first just to make sure.

45

"No Christmas for You!"

BELIEVE IT OR NOT, it was once a crime to celebrate Christmas in America. In 1659, the Puritans passed a law forbidding the observance of Christmas—a transgression that carried a fine of five shillings. Five shillings then is about $36 today. However, for a better perspective on the severity of the fine, keep in mind that five shillings was about two days' wages for a skilled craftsman of the day.

Boston lawmakers were particularly severe. Men in Boston, a strong bastion of the Protestant work ethic, were required to work every Christmas Day unless it fell on the Sabbath. A man could be dismissed from his job if he failed to show up for work on Christmas. And many employers required their employees to report for work at 5:00 a.m. to keep them from participating in any early-morning Christmas activities.

Children didn't have it much easier. A child who failed to attend school on Christmas Day faced expulsion.

The Christmas ban included the following:

- dancing
- musicals, pageants, cantatas, and other performances
- games
- singing
- caroling
- drinking
- any and all "cheerful celebrations"
- Christmas trees
- Christmas decorations
- traditional Christmas foods (such as mince pies and puddings)

Just in case some folks didn't get the message, town criers wandered about, calling out, "No Christmas, no Christmas!"

Why the severe approach to the holiday? The Puritans who settled in New England wanted to distance themselves from the celebrations associated with the Church of England, which had little to do with the birth of Christ and much to do with drinking and frivolity. So, the government instituted the 1659 ban, which remained in place for 22 years.

Even after the ban was revoked, it cast a long shadow over early American Christmases. It wasn't until the early 1800s that Christmas was celebrated on a large scale in cities like Boston.

47

Awesome
(AND OCCASIONALLY ILLEGAL)
Blossoms

CHERRY BLOSSOMS are a beautiful way to usher in the spirit of Christmas. To create your own cherry blossoms, break off a branch of a cherry tree at the beginning of Advent (about three and a half weeks before Christmas). Keep the branch in water in a warm room. The flowers should burst into bloom by Christmas Day.

Traditionally, cherry blossoms are regarded as symbols of good fortune, love, and friendship. And because their blooming is so brief (only a few days), they remind us of the fleeting nature of life and the need to make the most of each Christmas Day—and all the other days too.

Washington, DC, is famous for its Cherry Blossom Festival, but if you attend, beware. Picking one of *those* blossoms is viewed as vandalism of federal property, leading to a fine or even an arrest.

48

Tree-
MENDOUS LEGENDS

THE LEGENDS SURROUNDING the origins of the traditional Christmas tree are many, but the best resemblance to what is enjoyed in homes today dates to the late 1830s. In a German play known simply as *Paradise*, a fir tree hung with apples was used as a set piece. Reportedly inspired by the play, Prince Albert, the German husband of Queen Victoria, displayed a beautifully decorated tree—complete with an angel on top—in Windsor Castle.

The Illustrated London News carried a picture of the royal family gathered around their tree, which spurred the common folk to want trees of their own.

The trend soon crossed the Atlantic to the United States, and the Christmas tree became a staple of the holiday.

That Famous Poem

BY CLEMENT C. MOORE (PROBABLY)

WRITTEN IN 1822 by Clement C. Moore, "The Night Before Christmas" was originally titled "Account of a Visit from St. Nicholas." Moore created the poem for his six children as a holiday gift. He read his work aloud to the children and other assorted relatives gathered around the family fireplace. The poem so delighted its audience that one of the relatives (or possibly his housekeeper) submitted it to the *Sentinel*, a Troy, New York, newspaper. The paper first published the poem on December 23, 1823. (The poem was published anonymously at first. Moore, the son of a clergyman, officially claimed ownership for the piece in 1836.)

After Moore's name was linked to the piece, the children of Henry Livingston Jr. protested, claiming that their father had been reciting the poem since 1807. Meanwhile, it was discovered that Livingston Jr. was related to Clement C. Moore's wife. This roiled the troubled waters even more.

While the poem's authorship is disputed, there is no doubt about Moore's credentials as a writer. He earned a degree in classical literature from Columbia College (which accepted him at age 16). He spoke six languages and taught for decades at Protestant Episcopal Seminary in New York City. He published a variety of articles, poems, and political essays.

50

A Monk and His Math

MOST PEOPLE KNOW December 25 is probably not Jesus's actual birthdate. (Many historians believe Christ was born in the springtime.) There is also some confusion over the exact year of Jesus's birth, not just the day.

Why the uncertainty? You can point a finger at Dionysius Exiguus, a sixth-century monk who lived in what is present-day Romania. He was asked to create a Christian calendar to replace the pagan one used by the Romans.

Dionysius decided to start his calendar with Christ's birth. Unfortunately, he made several miscalculations. He based his work on the number of years served by each Roman emperor, counting back to the time of Christ. He stumbled when he got to Augustus, who reigned from 31 BCE to 14 CE.

The confused monk marked the reign as 27 BCE to 14 CE. The problem: During the first four years of his reign, Emperor Augustus was known as Octavian (his given name).

Dionysius either forgot about the name change, or he never knew about it.

Then the monk completely forgot the year zero. His calendar hopped from 1 BC to 1 CE, pruning an entire year from the document.

This five-year discrepancy is something we have lived with ever since. A lesson is here for all of us. Whether we are mechanics, monks, or millwrights, details do matter.

Xmas Marks the Spot?

IS THE TERM "XMAS" really a weapon in the alleged "war on Christmas" that we hear about every holiday season?

To some, the answer is yes. A 2018 *Christianity Today* article noted that nearly 6 in 10 people with evangelical beliefs (59 percent) find the use of Xmas instead of Christmas to be offensive.

Ironically, Xmas has been used by Christians and the church for hundreds of years, long before the term appeared in holiday advertisements and packaging. There was no intention to remove Christ from the holiday that celebrates him. The *X* stands for *chi*, the Greek letter that begins the word "Christ" or "Christos."

Constantine, the first Roman emperor to convert to Christianity, instructed his soldiers to display the letter on their shields before the Battle of Milvian Bridge.

The abbreviation also appeared in early Greek manuscripts of the New Testament.

The English version of the abbreviation dates back to at least 1021, when an Anglo-Saxon scribe shortened Christmas to "XPmas." (*X* and *P* denote *chi* and *rho*, the first two Greek letters of Christ, and Constantine combined them to create the "XP" symbol for Jesus. Eventually, the letter *P* was dropped.)

By the mid-1400s, churches were substituting *X* for Christ in their literature. By the 1500s, Webster's dictionary recognized "X-mas" as a common abbreviation. In the 1800s, writers like Samuel Taylor Coleridge were using X-mas or Xmas in their poems, essays, and stories.

Perhaps the renowned theologian R.C. Sproul explained it best: "The X in Christmas is used like the R in R.C. My given name at birth was Robert Charles, although before I was even taken home from the hospital, my parents called me by initials...and nobody seems to be too scandalized by that."

Sproul noted that *X* as an abbreviation for Christ came into use in our culture with no intent to show disrespect for the Son of God. "There's a long and sacred history of the use of X to symbolize the name of Christ," he asserted, "and from its origin, it has meant no disrespect."

So, perhaps the next time someone protests, "Let's put Christ back in Christmas," we can remind him or her that Christ has *always* been in Christmas. And he always will be.

How the Christmas
COOKIE CRUMBLES

HAVE YOU EVER left cookies for Santa on Christmas Eve? Many of today's families carry on this long-standing tradition with sugary treats either store bought or home-made along with a glass of milk.

"Cookies for a Claus" is a charming gesture, but have you ever wondered about its origins? Some scholars trace the practice to ancient Norse tales. However, the custom truly became widespread during the Depression in the United States. Parents encouraged their kids to leave treats for Santa—not to bribe him to leave them presents, but to express gratitude for *anything* they might receive during the challenging economic times.

Perhaps understanding a bit more about this tradition will help us all be more thankful the next time we eat a cookie or leave one for Santa.

Thinking Outside
THE BOX ABOUT BOXING DAY

MANY PEOPLE KNOW that Boxing Day falls on the day after Christmas. And they know it has nothing to do with pugilism.

However, some folks are under the mistaken impression that the name of the holiday sprang from the custom of boxing up unwanted Christmas gifts and returning them to the store for a refund or an exchange.

In reality, the day marks a tradition dating to the Middle Ages. In the United Kingdom, Boxing Day was the occasion when churches opened their "alms boxes" (or collection boxes) and distributed funds to the poor. Moreover, servants were given Boxing Day off so they could spend a belated Christmas with their friends and family after having to work on Christmas Day. In medieval times, the money was distributed in hollow clay pots with a slit in the top. (The pots had to be broken open to retrieve the money.) The pots were shaped like a pig, and they earned the nickname "piggies," perhaps the inspiration for piggy banks.

This day of benevolence was greatly appreciated by the less fortunate, as many of them had to pay their rent on Christmas Day. (Christmas was known as a "quarter day," one of the four days of the year on which major payments were due.)

A Christmas Tale

AS GOOD AS GOLD

WHY DO MILLIONS of people hang stockings at Christmastime? Why not some other article of clothing?

Perhaps the answer comes from good old Saint Nicholas himself.

One of the many stories about Saint Nicholas is the kindness he extended to three daughters of a poor family. The family's daughters wanted to get married but couldn't, as they had no dowries. (And in those days, a woman with no prospects of marriage was doomed to a life of poverty and shame.) Nicholas heard of their plight, and, under the cover of night, he tossed three bags of gold down the family chimney—where they landed neatly in the girls' stockings, which they had hung to dry by the fire.

Another version of the stocking story features Saint Nicholas dropping gold balls down the family's chimney. The balls landed in the stockings. In yet another variation on the theme, Nicholas tossed the gold balls through an open window, and they rolled right up to the amazed father's feet.

A Very Dickensian Christmas

WHEN CHARLES DICKENS penned *A Christmas Carol* in 1843, he crafted a timeless story. His tale of a tight-fisted man who learns Christmas's true meaning continues to resonate with readers. Dickens understood how money can affect one's life. His family was once imprisoned for debt, and he wrote *A Christmas Carol* in hopes of forestalling financial disaster after one of his novels failed to sell well.

The following quote from Dickens offers a glimpse into the spirit behind his famous story:

> "I have always thought of Christmas time, when it has come round, as a good time; a kind, forgiving, charitable time; the only time I know of, in the long calendar of the year, when men and women seem by one consent to open their shut-up hearts freely, and to think of people below them as if they really were fellow passengers to the grave, and not another race of creatures bound on other journeys."

It's fascinating to compare the quote above to the quote below from Fred, Scrooge's nephew, in the book itself:

> "But I am sure I have always thought of Christmas time...as a good time; a kind, forgiving, charitable, pleasant time: the only time I know of, in the long calendar of the year, when men and women seem by one consent to open their shut-up hearts freely..."

One Good King

LIKE MANY FAVORITE Christmas songs, "Good King Wenceslas," written in 1853 by British hymn writer John Mason Neale, celebrates a real person. The song, set to the tune of a carol from the 1300s ("The Time Is Near for Flowering"), portrays the story of a kind man who ventures out into a storm on the day after Christmas (known in some places as St. Stephen's Day) to help some of his needy neighbors.

The song's hero was a real man, Wenceslaus I, the Duke of Bohemia, who ruled from 924 to 935. His reign ended when he was assassinated by his own brother, Boleslav the Cruel. Wenceslas was loved by his subjects for his many acts of charity, such as the one from the song. After his death, he was posthumously declared a king, and he eventually earned sainthood. He is the patron saint of the Czech Republic.

How About a
CHRISTMAS MARATHON?

THE THOUGHT OF completing a marathon on Christmas appeals to very few, even to hard-core runners. But if the marathon involves 24 hours of enjoying a classic Christmas film, the participation rate goes way up—to the tune of more than 50 million viewers.

For more than 20 years, viewers have been tuning to TBS to watch the *A Christmas Story* marathon, enjoying the adventures of Ralphie Parker (played by Peter Billingsley) and his friends.

Turner Network Television kicked off the marathon in 1997. The show switched to sister station TBS in 2004.

If you are a fan of the 1983 film, you know that young Ralphie really wants a Red Ryder BB Gun (a real toy that first came to market in 1938). He mentions the gun 28 times over the course of the movie. That's once every 3 minutes and 20 seconds. If you were to watch all 12 viewings of the movie marathon, you'd hear Ralphie pine for his gun 336 times.

O Little Town of Bethlehem:

A POST-WAR SONG OF HEALING

AFTER THE CIVIL WAR, Phillips Brooks, a Philadelphia rector, felt he needed rest and a new perspective. He decided to spend Christmas 1865 in the Holy Land.

Once there, he borrowed a horse and rode through the quiet countryside from Jerusalem to Bethlehem, where he participated in the Church of the Nativity's five-hour Christmas Eve celebration. (Locals warned him of thieves, but he didn't worry. Not after the four bloody years he had witnessed.)

The night sky was clear and full of stars as Brooks rode into Bethlehem. He was awestruck to be riding through the place of Jesus's birth. Once he returned to Philadelphia, he struggled to explain the life-changing experience to his congregation. Then, three years later, while prepping for his 1868 Christmas service, he said the lyrics for a song came to him almost automatically.

He might have said the lyrics were "downloaded" into his brain, had he known what the word meant. He shared his poem with church organist Lewis Redner, who wrote the melody with an ear toward a performance by the church's children's choir. On December 27, 1868, the choir performed the song, beginning with these fondly remembered lyrics:

> O little town of Bethlehem
> How still we see thee lie
> Above thy deep and dreamless sleep
> The silent stars go by.
>
> Yet in thy dark streets shineth
> The everlasting Light.
> The hopes and fears of all the years
> Are met in thee tonight.

DID YOU KNOW?

Philips Brooks was more than a songwriter. He was a Boston-born Episcopal minister who earned a Doctor of Divinity degree from Oxford, taught at Yale, and publicly opposed slavery during the years of the Civil War. To many, he was more famous for his preaching than his songwriting. The first volume of his collected sermons, published in 1878, sold more than 200,000 copies in the first year of publication. Those sermons are still valued by scholars and parishioners today.

59

The Christmas Card

THAT INSPIRED A MOVIE

ANY ASPIRING WRITER should be inspired by the saga of Philip Van Doren Stern. Stern wrote a short story titled "The Greatest Gift," which he tried to sell to publishers—for years and years. After collecting a stack of rejection notices, Stern did the 1940s version of self-publishing. He decided to make a Christmas gift of his story.

In 1943, he printed 200 copies of his 21-page saga and sent it as a Christmas card to his family and friends. Stern reasoned that if he couldn't sell his story, he should give it away.

Somehow (perhaps it was one of those miracles that seem to occur at Christmastime), "The Greatest Gift" ended up in the hands of David Hempstead, a producer at RKO Pictures. Hempstead loved the story and offered Stern $10,000 for the movie rights. To put that number in perspective, $10,000 in 1943 equals more than $148,000 in today's dollars.

Hempstead then shared the work with filmmaker Frank Capra, who said he had been looking for such a story "all my life." However, Capra felt the title wasn't quite right. He wanted to change it.

Three years later (in 1946), Capra released a film adaptation of "The Greatest Gift." His new title? *It's a Wonderful Life*, starring James Stewart, Donna Reed, and Lionel Barrymore.

A Toothy Christmas Wish

CHRISTMAS HAS INSPIRED a variety of songs from the sacred to the silly. One favorite from the latter category is the 1948 hit "All I Want for Christmas Is My Two Front Teeth."

This well-known novelty song was written by Don Gardner in 1946, and it was first performed nationally on Perry Como's radio show by an obscure vocal group known as the Satisfiers. However, that performance was less than satisfying to some listeners, and the song didn't really catch on.

Two years later, Spike Jones and His City Slickers crafted a zany version of the song on the RCA Victor label. George Rock, trumpet player and vocalist for the band, portrayed a child longing for his two front teeth so that he could wish everyone "Merry Christmas" without lisping. Even though he was a hulk of a man who played college football, Rock made a convincing child, and the song was a huge hit. The single was certified gold (sales of more than 500,000 copies), and it reached No. 1 on the *Billboard* pop chart.

Christmas in Mayberry

WHEN PEOPLE THINK of family-friendly television, *The Andy Griffith Show* often comes to mind. The show, which aired on CBS from 1960 to 1968, was as wholesome and down-home as the meals prepared by Aunt Bee.

That's why it's somewhat surprising that out of the series' 249 episodes, only one centered on Christmas. Titled "Christmas Story," it aired on December 19, 1960, during the series' first year.

The show's story line perfectly captured the spirit of Christmas. On Christmas Eve, Sheriff Andy Taylor (played by Andy Griffith) releases the prisoners from the local jail so that they can spend Christmas with their loved ones. He makes them promise to return the day after Christmas to complete their sentences.

Soon, Sam Muggins, one of the released prisoners is returned to the sheriff on charges of selling bootleg whisky. Sheriff Taylor has no choice but to re-incarcerate Muggins, but he is still determined to give his prisoner a Christmas to remember. So, with help from his son, Opie, Deputy Barney Fife, Aunt Bee, and girlfriend, Ellie Walker, the sheriff throws a Christmas party at the jail, inviting Muggins's wife and two children to join them.

Barney (played by Don Knotts) dresses up like Santa Claus, and Andy and Ellie perform a reverent duet of "Away in a Manger," with the sheriff accompanying on guitar.

Christmas at the Movies

FOR MANY AT CHRISTMASTIME, watching a classic holiday film is part of the holiday tradition. The choice of which movie is a tough one, but perhaps the list below will help. A few years ago, the American Film Institute compiled its list of the best holiday films of the past 100 years.

Here are the top 10:

1. It's a Wonderful Life (1946)
2. Holiday Inn (1942)
3. White Christmas (1954)
4. The Bishop's Wife (1947)
5. A Christmas Carol (1951)
6. Miracle on 34th Street (1947)
7. Christmas in Connecticut (1945)
8. Meet Me in St. Louis (1944)
9. Going My Way (1944)
10. The Shop Around the Corner (1940)

TOP 10

FILMS

Looks a Lot Like Snow

IF YOU ARE A FAN of classic Christmas movies, you probably know about a few of Hollywood's tricks to bring winter scenes to life without the complications of shooting in actual snowstorms.

It's a Wonderful Life was filmed in the summer of 1946 during a heat wave. At one point, director Frank Capra had to cease filming for a whole day because of the high temperatures.

The heat is one reason that you can see star Jimmy Steward sweating profusely in several scenes. It wasn't method acting; it was the 90-degree heat.

In such weather, of course, using real snow was out of the question. Many people think that Capra used painted cornflakes as snow, as that was the go-to solution in Hollywood in the 1940s. But Capra didn't like the noise created by the fake flakes. (If you've ever spilled breakfast cereal on the floor and walked through it, you can probably sympathize.)

This made dialogue hard to hear. (Many filmmakers dubbed in the dialogue later.) However, Capra wanted the dialogue to take place in the moment so it would sound and feel real.

Capra (who earned a degree in chemical engineering) and special-effects supervisor Russell Shearman decided to create a better snowflake, give or take a few thousand. The duo mixed sugar, soap flakes, and water with a fire-fighting chemical called Foamite. The resulting "snow" looked great on film, and it didn't crackle when trod upon. In all, it took about 6,000 gallons of the stuff to transform summer in California to Christmas in Bedford Falls.

While the film did not win any traditional Oscars, the Motion Picture Academy gave it a Technical Award for the snow, which was pumped at high pressure through a wind machine to create the look of fresh flakes falling on trees and streets and drifting against buildings. Quite a feat, considering that Bedford Falls occupied four full acres and included 75 stores and buildings, a tree-lined parkway, a 300-yard Main Street, 20 full-grown oak trees, a factory district, and residential areas.

Is "The Christmas Song"
THE CHRISTMAS SONG?

"THE CHRISTMAS SONG" (sometimes referred to as "Chestnuts Roasting on an Open Fire") is one of the hottest holiday tunes ever. In more ways than one.

Nat King Cole made the song famous, but it was born on a hot summer day in 1945 thanks to the talents of Robert Wells and Mel "The Velvet Fog" Tormé.

Tormé said he was inspired by a few lines scrawled in pencil on a spiral pad on Wells's piano. The lines included the now-famous imagery of chestnuts roasting, Jack Frost nipping, and people dressed like Eskimos. However, Wells wasn't thinking of a song when he wrote the words. He was simply surrounding himself with winter elements in an effort to cool off. "I thought that maybe if I could just write down a few lines of wintry verse, I could physiologically get an edge over this heat," Wells explained.

But those few lines inspired Tormé, who wrote all of the music and worked with Wells, a frequent writing partner, to round out the lyrics. The whole process took only 40 minutes.

The following June, the Nat King Cole Trio became the first act to record the song. Cole provided the trademark vocals and played piano, supported by Oscar Moore on guitar and Johnny Miller on bass. But you probably haven't heard this version. It wasn't made public until 1989, when it was released, *accidentally*, on a multi-artist compilation from Rhino Records.

Later in 1946, Cole recorded the song again, joined by a small string section. This version became a blockbuster hit, climbing both the pop and R&B charts.

But Cole wasn't finished with the song. He recorded it again in 1953, joined by conductor Nelson Riddle and a full orchestra. The year 1961 saw Cole in the studio yet again, with another orchestra, this time under the direction of Ralph Carmichael. *This* is the version that many audiophiles consider definitive.

Cole passed away in 1965, and Tormé died in 1999, but a host of other artists have kept the beloved recording alive. According to BMI, it is the most-performed Christmas song. Artists who have done the song, many times and many ways, include Stevie Wonder, Frank Sinatra, Perry Como, Christina Aguilera, Michael Bublé, Bing Crosby, Lauren Daigle, and the duet of Justin Bieber and Usher. The song has also made multiple appearances on the large and small screen, from the film *Catch Me if You Can* to the classic TV series *The Simpsons*.

Clearly, there is something special about this cool Christmas song, written on a hot summer day.

A Bittersweet Christmas Hit

MANY FAVORITE HOLIDAY SONGS are full of cheer and celebration, but a beloved song for many strikes a tone that is both mournful and hopeful. "Have Yourself a Merry Little Christmas" was written for a scene in the 1944 movie musical *Meet Me in St. Louis*. Fans of the film will recall that Judy Garland sings the lyrics to her sister in an effort to bolster her spirits as the family faces the challenge of moving away from their hometown.

During the filming, Garland and director Vincente Minnelli struggled with the song, written by Hugh Martin. At first, Martin refused to revise his lyrics, which he felt captured the sometimes-bittersweet tone of the holidays. Tom Drake, another of the film's stars, took a harder stance than Garland and Minnelli. He called Martin "stupid" and warned, "You're gonna foul up your life if you don't write another verse of that song!"

Drake's warning worked. Thirteen years later, the song got another injection of hope. Frank Sinatra wanted to record the song, but he hoped to strike an even brighter tone than Garland. (The title of Sinatra's album was *A Jolly Christmas*, and he reportedly asked Martin to "jolly up" the song for him.) So Martin tweaked more of his words.

Years later, Martin would confess that his original lyrics were "hysterically lugubrious."

Washington Irving
REBRANDS CHRISTMAS

EARLY NINETEENTH-CENTURY America was marred by class conflicts and unrest. Unemployment rates were high, and the disenfranchised often expressed their displeasure via riots and rowdy protests. Things sometimes became so bad that the police had to respond.

Enter bestselling author Washington Irving. In 1819, he published *The Sketchbook of Geoffrey Crayon, Gent.*, a short-story collection centered on the celebration of Christmas in an English manor house. In Irving's world, the squire of the manor invited peasants into his home to celebrate the holiday with him and his family. In stark contrast to what was happening in American society, Irving's characters mingled joyfully, respectfully, and, it seemed, effortlessly. Christmas brought everyone together, erasing the lines of wealth and social status.

The book was not based on some magical Christmas dinner that the author attended. Instead, Irving invented his own traditions. He described people who interacted the way God intended. He envisioned a Christmas that transcended the status quo, a better Christmas. And that's what he presented to the world.

In the years after the book's publication, Americans embraced Christmas in a new way. It was no longer a rowdy party. It was now a day of faith and family.

It's a Wonderful Life

(ESPECIALLY AT CHRISTMASTIME)

STARRING JIMMY STEWART as a man who attempts suicide on Christmas Eve, this classic Frank Capra film is a staple of Christmas viewing.

However, when *It's a Wonderful Life* was released in 1946, it was considered a commercial flop despite its five Academy Award nominations. It didn't come close to reaching its $6.3 million break-even point.

One reason the movie was so expensive was its elaborate set, which took up four full acres. The set featured 75 stores and other buildings, 20 full-grown oak trees, factories, residential areas, and a Main Street that stretched 300 yards (the length of three football fields).

The poor box office performance put Capra in a half-million-dollar hole, and he was barely able to finance his next film.

Perhaps one reason for the film's rough first couple of years was that the FBI issued a memo citing *It's a Wonderful Life* as "Communist infiltration of the motion picture industry." The feds objected to the movie's "rather obvious attempts to discredit bankers by casting Lionel Barrymore as a 'scrooge-type' so that he would be the most hated man in the picture." This was a "common trick used by Communists" according to J. Edgar Hoover and his associates.

But the film eventually found its niche as a recurring TV special, and later on home video. The TV success came about in a strange way. In 1974, the film's copyright lapsed, making it available, royalty-free, to anyone who wanted to broadcast it for the next 20 years.

It's a Wonderful Life, with its message of how one person can touch the lives of many others, has been recognized by the American Film Institute as one of the 100 best American films ever made—placing No. 1 on AFI's list of most inspirational films of all time.

Capra, Stewart, and Reed boast impressive resumes, but all three cited *It's a Wonderful Life* as their favorite movie. Capra went so far as to say, "I thought it was the greatest film I ever made. Better yet, I thought it was the greatest film anybody ever made."

68

A Subway Song

OF CHRISTMAS

"SANTA CLAUS IS COMIN' TO TOWN" is one of the jolliest tunes of the Christmas season. First made famous by Eddie Cantor in 1934, it's been recorded by a variety of artists, from Bruce Springsteen to Frank Sinatra to Mariah Carey to Justin Bieber.

Fans of the snappy song might be surprised to learn that it sprang from a time of grief in its creator's life. Lyricist James "Haven" Gillespie was a vaudevillian-turned-songwriter whose career had stalled. In fact, the invitation to compose a Christmas song for Cantor came just after Gillespie's brother died.

At first, Gillespie declined the assignment. He felt too grief-stricken to write. However, during a subway ride, Gillespie was reminded of his childhood with his brother, and how their mother had encouraged good behavior by reminding them, "Santa is watching you!"

In 15 short minutes, Gillespie came up with the lyrics. Then he called on composer John Coots to create the music. They delivered the song to Cantor, and it became a huge hit less than 24 hours after Cantor first performed it on his radio show.

I'm Dreaming

OF A BLUE CHRISTMAS

"WHITE CHRISTMAS" is a signature holiday song for many, but a selection about a Christmas of another color has made its mark as well.

"Blue Christmas," a melancholy song of unrequited love, was first made famous by country artist Ernest Tubb in 1949. However, a follow-up recording really put the song (written by Billy Hayes and Jay W. Johnson) on the musical map.

Elvis Presley cut his distinctive version in 1957 as part of his LP *Elvis' Christmas Album*. The "King's" rendition inspired a host of other artists to record the song—from the Beach Boys to Billy Idol to Celine Dion to Jon Bon Jovi.

The song returned to its country roots in 2008, when Martina McBride recorded a "virtual duet" with Elvis, for the concept project *Christmas Duets*. (The Elvis/Martina duet also appears on McBride's 2013 release *The Classic Christmas Album*.)

70

Peanuts for Christmas

ALONG WITH *It's a Wonderful Life, A Charlie Brown Christmas* has endured as a timeless holiday classic. The first of many prime-time TV specials based on the classic *Peanuts* comic strip, Charlie Brown's Christmas story premiered on December 9, 1965—right after an episode of *Gilligan's Island*. Fully half of America's TV sets were tuned in to witness Charlie Brown's search for a tree for his school play—and, in the process, the true meaning of Christmas. In the ensuing years, it has become an annual staple of the holiday season.

The show was somewhat controversial, as the producer and lead animator objected to the biblical text from the New Testament book of Luke being part of the special. However, *Peanuts* creator Charles Schulz insisted that the biblical material remain.

After the broadcast, *The New York World-Telegram* proclaimed, "Linus' reading of the story of the Nativity was, quite simply, the dramatic highlight of the season."

THE GOSPEL ACCORDING TO LUKE (AND LINUS)

Here is the text spoken by Linus van Pelt in *A Charlie Brown Christmas* (from Luke 2:8-14, King James Version):

There were in the same country shepherds abiding in the field, keeping watch over their flock by night.

And, lo, the angel of the Lord came upon them, and the glory of the Lord shone round about them: and they were sore afraid.

And the angel said unto them, Fear not: for, behold, I bring you good tidings of great joy, which shall be to all people.

For unto you is born this day in the city of David a Saviour, which is Christ the Lord.

And this shall be a sign unto you; Ye shall find the babe wrapped in swaddling clothes, lying in a manger.

And suddenly there was with the angel a multitude of the heavenly host praising God, and saying,

Glory to God in the highest, and on earth peace, good will toward men.

71

Make Some Noise
FOR "SILENT NIGHT"

PERHAPS THE FAVORITE religious Christmas song of them all, "Silent Night" is a collaboration between a young Austrian priest named Father Josef Mohr (lyrics) and a headmaster named Franz Gruber (music).

Written in German ("Stille Nacht"), the carol was first performed at the Church of St. Nicholas in Oberndorf, Austria, on Christmas Eve 1818. According to Austria's Silent Night Society, the composition's gentle signature melody sprung partly out of necessity. The Church of St. Nicholas's organ was broken, so Mohr and Gruber crafted a song that could be accompanied on the guitar.

According to several stories about the song, Mohr first tried to fix the organ but failed. He began to pray for a solution. While in prayer, he recalled a holiday poem he had written years previously. He'd shared the poem with a few friends but never sought to publish it.

He retrieved the poem from a desk drawer and headed for the home of Gruber, a friend and a noted composer. With only a few hours to work, Mohr and Gruber completed the song and quickly taught it to the church choir. Accompanied by Gruber on the guitar, the choir performed the fledgling song, which filled the church and the hearts of the congregation.

The first English translation appeared in 1863. It's now been translated into more than 140 languages.

Jingle Bells

IN OUTER SPACE

ALTHOUGH IT'S a Christmas favorite, the dashing song "Jingle Bells" was originally written for *another* holiday. Circa 1857, James Lord Pierpont, an organist for a church in Savannah, Georgia, wrote the song (originally titled "One Horse Open Sleigh") for his Sunday school class's Thanksgiving celebration. It was so well received that Pierpont revived it for the church's Christmas festivities the following month, renaming it "Jingle Bells" and publishing it officially for the first time.

This song has historical significance, as it is the first carol to be broadcast from outer space. On December 16, 1965, the Gemini 6 astronauts played the song on bells and a harmonica that they had snuck onboard their spacecraft. They also reported seeing Santa Claus while traveling in space. Mission control responded, "You're too much, Six."

Incidentally, while most sources state that Pierpont wrote the song while living in Georgia, residents of Medford, Massachusetts, insist he wrote the classic while living in New England. Debate still rages today about the song's birthplace.

73

Carey Caroling

FOR MILLIONS

WHAT IS YOUR all-time favorite Christmas song? Is it one of the classics or something contemporary? Christmas music is a matter of taste, but, by at least one measure, the No. 1 Christmas song of all time is one that might surprise you.

The song celebrated its twenty-fourth anniversary during Christmas 2018 by setting a one-day streaming record on Spotify on Christmas Eve. Its title? "All I Want for Christmas Is You," cowritten and recorded by Mariah Carey in 1994. Christmas Eve 2018 saw the song played 10.8 million times on Spotify. Carey's song broke the record set by rapper XXXTentacion, whose song "SAD!" logged 10.4 million "plays" the day after his death in June 2018.

The streaming record was not a surprise to Carey's fans. "All I Want for Christmas Is You" had been topping the holiday charts every year since its release. The song reflects the artist's love for the Christmas season in general and Christmas music in particular. "I love the holidays," she told the press. "I've sung Christmas songs since I was a little girl. I used to go Christmas caroling. I wrote it just out of love for Christmas…and really loving Christmas music."

Christmas in Phoenix,
BY THE SWIMMING POOL

IN 1940, while sitting poolside in Phoenix, Arizona, Irving Berlin penned a song titled "White Christmas," which was sung to the world for the first time on Christmas Day, 1941, by Bing Crosby on the NBC radio program *Kraft Music Hall.*

Crosby recorded the song in May 1942—and again in 1947 after the original master recording was damaged.

With sales of more than 100 million units, the song is recognized by both Guinness and ItsRanked as the No. 1 Christmas song (and No. 1 single of any kind) of all time. If all this weren't enough, "White Christmas" was also voted the Academy Award for Best Original Song (showcased in the 1942 film *Holiday Inn*).

75

The Perfect Christmas Gift?

DO YOU HAVE a favorite Christmas story or folk tale? For many, the all-time classic is O. Henry's "The Gift of the Magi," originally published in 1906. Laced with poignant irony, this story portrays two newlyweds too poor to buy Christmas gifts for each other. Ultimately, the lovers sacrifice their respective prized possessions so that they can purchase a gift. The message of this classic still rings true today: The gifts we treasure most are the ones that are given from the heart, with no thought of their cost.

This story's message becomes even more poignant when one considers its author. O. Henry is a pen name of William Sydney Porter. Porter began writing in the late 1880s but got truly serious about the craft when he found himself with hours of time to kill. You see, Porter, whose mother died when he was only three, was imprisoned in 1898 for embezzling funds from an Austin, Texas, bank where he worked as a clerk. (To this day, disturbing questions remain about his guilt, but he was sentenced to a five-year term nonetheless.)

Porter, who had a wife and daughter at the time, fled to Honduras to avoid jail. However, he returned to the States when his wife was diagnosed with a terminal illness. He spent three years in jail, where he wrote feverishly to support his daughter, Margaret. He published 12 stories while incarcerated. After serving his time, Porter moved from Texas to New York, where he was hired by the *New York World* to write a story a week. He worked for the paper for three years, and, as a side hustle, published several short-story collections. "The Gift of the Magi" is from 1906's *The Four Million*. Because he was ashamed and embarrassed by his criminal record, Porter wrote under the pen name Olivier Henry, which was later shortened to O. Henry. He would write almost 600 stories in total.

One of Henry's last stories, 1910's "The Ransom of Red Chief," is perhaps his best known. It was adapted into several films, including 1911's *The Ransom of Red Chief*, 1962's *Business People*, and 1986's *Ruthless People* (starring Danny DeVito and Bette Midler).

Henry is also credited for creating the character the Cisco Kid. He lived to see silent-film adaptations of three of his stories before he passed away in June 1910 at age 48.

DID YOU KNOW?

O. Henry's first published story was titled "Whistling Dick's Christmas Stocking."

Wrong Number, Right Idea

ON CHRISTMAS EVE 1955 at the Continental Air Defense Command (CONAD), US Air Force Colonel Harry Shoup received a call on the "red phone." That meant, most likely, a call from the Pentagon, perhaps about a national emergency. Perhaps an air attack from the Soviet Union.

Instead, Colonel Shoup found himself on the phone with a young girl. "Are you really Santa Claus?" she asked.

Instead of scolding the girl, the bemused commander played along. He reported that he was indeed Santa. He reviewed the girl's wish list with her and encouraged her to leave food for both Santa and his reindeer.

The phone call was no prank, although that's what Shoup originally believed. A Colorado Springs newspaper ran a Sears Roebuck ad encouraging kids to call a number and speak with Santa Claus. "Hey, Kiddies!" the ad invited. "Call me on my private phone, and I will talk to you personally any time day or night."

However, a typographical error resulted in CONAD's hotline number (not the number for "Sears Santa") being shared with thousands of readers. (At the time, CONAD's major mission was monitoring the skies for a possible nuclear attack by the Soviet Union.)

Flash-forward 65 years. Today, NORAD Tracks Santa receives about 155,000 phone calls each Christmas season while also drawing almost 11 million unique visitors to its website. At press time, the program had 1.8 million Facebook followers, 382,000 YouTube views, and 177,000 Twitter followers.

The program is run by the US and Canadian militaries (via the North American Aerospace Defense Command). The website www.noradsanta.org offers updates in a variety of languages, and updates are also posted on Facebook, Twitter, and Instagram. In 2017, Alexa (Amazon's voice-activated computer service) began relaying NORAD Tracks Santa updates through its Echo device.

Even with all the high-tech options, NORAD's phones ring nonstop each holiday season. Children from North America (as well as those as far away as Japan and the United Kingdom) call to learn Santa's current location and his ETA at their homes. Volunteers (numbering about 1,500 each season) receive about 80 calls an hour, according to NORAD spokesman Captain Chase MacFarland.

Many callers want to know what kind of cookies or other treats to leave for Santa. Volunteers are instructed to tell them that anything will work. "Santa's not a picky eater," MacFarland explains.

DID YOU KNOW?

The toll-free number for NORAD Tracks Santa is 877-Hi NORAD (or 877-446-6723).

A Very Hospitable Holiday

ALMOST EVERYONE loves spending Christmas at home, either our own abodes or that of family or friends. But what if you or someone you love ends up in the hospital (or some other care facility) at Christmastime?

It's a challenge, but there is no reason to be disconnected from the love and spirit of the season. With a little resourcefulness, you can bring the wonder of Christmas to a hospital room. Here are a few suggestions:

Make merry music. Music can be therapeutic and uplifting for almost anyone dealing with an injury, illness, or other health challenge. You can sing carols or play favorite Christmas music on a laptop, smartphone, or other device. Of course, you should check with facility staff to make sure you are complying with guidelines and being sensitive to other patients.

Have tree, will travel. What's a Christmas celebration without a tree? It's probably not practical to bring a full-sized natural tree into relatively cramped quarters, but a variety of artificial trees are beautiful, easily portable, and small enough to fit on a nightstand or corner of even the smallest room.

To decorate the tree, consider asking guests (especially kids) to create homemade decorations.

Ham it up. We have all heard the jokes about hospital food, but many hospitals and other care facilities serve a traditional ham or turkey dinner that is surprisingly tasty. If you would rather celebrate with a home-cooked or catered meal, ask the staff for guidelines regarding dietary restrictions, food allergies, and so on.

Get carded. Christmas cards bring beauty and encouragement to any holiday celebration, whether it's at home or the hospital. Display some of your best cards on the walls of your hospital room. Hang a few from your hospital-friendly tree. Encourage kids to create homemade cards, and let them read a few cards as part of the celebration.

Picture this. Photos can bring a touch of home to even the most sterile setting. Display a few framed photos around the hospital room. A tech-savvy friend or family member can probably create a photo montage on a laptop or other device.

Yes, there is no place like home for the holidays, but part of the wonder of Christmas is discovering that "home" is more than a place. It's the spirit created when people gather anywhere to celebrate, worship, reminisce, and laugh together.

Fixing the Date...
AND MORE

WHEN WAS THE FIRST official celebration of Christmas held? There is no way to know for sure, but in 125 CE, Telesphorus, the eighth bishop of Rome, declared that church services be held to honor "the Nativity of our Lord and Savior." Because no one was sure when Jesus was born, these services were often held in September during the Jewish Feast of Trumpets (known as Rosh Hashanah today). Eventually, January 6 became the date, in accordance with the modern-day Epiphany. The lack of consensus on a date reflects that the celebration was not a major priority in the early days of Christianity.

In 274, the winter solstice fell on December 25. Roman Emperor Aurelian proclaimed the date *Natalis Solis Invicti*, or the birth of the invincible sun. Christians didn't like the sun getting more attention than the Son but felt powerless to do much. They liked the idea of a celebration tied to the solstices but didn't like following Rome's lead on matters of religious significance.

By the year 320, Pope Julius I had grown tired of seeing Jesus's birth celebrated so haphazardly. For no apparent reason, he specified December 25 as Christ's official birthday. Many ignored the proclamation and continued to celebrate whenever.

By the fourth century, however, the Roman Empire had begun to convert to Christianity, but Christmas was still connected to Saturnalia, a popular Roman festival.

In 325, Constantine the Great, a recent Christian convert, declared Christmas to be "an immovable feast," to be celebrated on December 25. People celebrated with wild parties and then attended Christmas services to repent.

This disconnect between Christians' behavior and the true meaning of the holiday continued for hundreds of years. In fact, "how to properly celebrate Christmas" was an official party plank that led to the overthrowing of the English monarchy in 1649 when Oliver Cromwell led a rebellion against King Charles I.

Cromwell was a Puritan who carried the title Lord Protector. He believed in law and order and wanted to create a civil democracy. He banned all Christmas festivities. If you were caught singing carols or celebrating in the streets, you were arrested, fined, and jailed.

When the "Law and Order" era ended and the English monarchy resumed (in the 1660s), Christmas made a comeback.

The Christmas Seals
OF APPROVAL

THE FAMOUS ADHESIVE labels that decorate millions of holiday letters and packages were first printed and sold in Denmark early in the 20th century. In 1904, Danish postal clerk Einar Holbøll created seals to raise money to fight tuberculosis. The postmaster (and the king of Denmark himself) approved the effort. More than 4 million seals were sold that year.

Three years later, Emily Bissell introduced the concept in the United States after reading about Christmas Seals. She designed and printed her seals and sold them from a table in a Delaware post office for a penny each.

At the time, tuberculosis was America's leading cause of death. Doctors were seeing success when treating the illness in special hospitals called sanatoriums. One of these facilities, located in Delaware, faced closure unless it could raise $300 to continue operating. One of the facility's doctors shared his plight with his cousin: Emily Bissell. Bissell, a veteran fund-raiser, went into action. President Theodore Roosevelt endorsed her efforts, which amassed more than 10 times the original fund-raising goal. That means that Bissell and her team of volunteers sold more than 300,000 seals.

Christmas Seals went national in 1908.

Christmas Is... Amazing,

EXTRAVAGANT GENEROSITY

TALES OF EXTREME GENEROSITY abound at Christmastime, but the unofficial champion of the grand generous gesture is publishing magnate James Gordon Bennett Jr. After a satisfying breakfast back in 1876, Bennett left his waiter a Christmas tip of $6,000. That's more than $112,000 in today's dollars.

Then there is the Houston company that gave all its employees a Christmas gift they will never forget.

In 2015, Hilcorp, a Houston-based oil and natural gas exploration and production company, gave each employee a $100,000 Christmas bonus. All 1,380 staff members received the bonus, regardless of position or seniority.

That grand Christmas gesture was not a one-off for Hilcorp. In 2010, the company met a five-year goal, and each worker was treated to the choice of a $50,000 car or $35,000 in cash.

Not surprisingly, Hilcorp is a fixture on the "Fortune 100 Best Companies to Work For" list.

> "NO ONE IS USELESS
> IN THIS WORLD WHO LIGHTENS
> THE BURDEN OF ANOTHER."
>
> — CHARLES DICKENS

A Christmas Eve

SCRIPTURE READING...FROM SPACE

ONE OF THE GREATEST Christmas Eve broadcasts originated from outer space. On December 24, 1968, an estimated 25 percent of the world's population heard a reading of Genesis 1:1-12 (KJV), courtesy of Apollo 8 astronauts Frank Borman (mission commander), James Lovell (command module pilot), and William Anders (lunar module pilot). On live TV, they took turns reading the following:

> In the beginning God created the heaven and the earth. And the earth was without form, and void; and darkness was upon the face of the deep. And the Spirit of God moved upon the face of the waters. And God said, Let there be light: and there was light. And God saw the light, that it was good: and God divided the light from the darkness.
>
> And God called the light Day, and the darkness he called Night. And the evening and the morning were the first day. And God said, Let there be a firmament in the midst of the waters,

and let it divide the waters from the waters. And God made the firmament, and divided the waters which were under the firmament from the waters which were above the firmament: and it was so. And God called the firmament Heaven. And the evening and the morning were the second day.

And God said, Let the waters under the heavens be gathered together unto one place, and let the dry land appear: and it was so. And God called the dry land Earth; and the gathering together of the waters he called the Seas: and God saw that it was good.

After the Scripture reading, Borman concluded, "From the crew of Apollo 8, we close with good night, good luck, a Merry Christmas, and God bless all of you—all of you on the good Earth."

Apollo 8's main mission was to circle the moon (10 times in 24 hours), scouting the planned lunar landing of the Apollo 11 mission. The team photographed the moon and the earth, including the first image of the "earthrise," a view of our planet that had not been captured before.

Many people were captivated by the holiday reading. Pope Paul VI later told Borman, "I have spent my entire life trying to say to the world what you did on Christmas Eve."

A Time to Hope

IN 1897, an eight-year-old girl named Virginia O'Hanlon wrote to the *New York Sun*, asking if Santa Claus truly existed—and noting her friends' skepticism about the prospects. Her father told her, "If you see it in the *Sun*, it's so." This prompted Virginia to write a letter to the paper, in careful cursive: "Please tell me the truth; is there a Santa Claus?"

The *Sun* printed a response on September 21, 1897, which affirmed, "Yes, Virginia, there is a Santa Claus. He exists as certainly as love and generosity and devotion exist, and you know that they abound and give to our life the highest beauty and joy."

Sun editorial writer Francis Pharcellus Church went on to say, "There is a veil covering the unseen world, which not the strongest man, nor even the united strength of all the strongest men that ever lived, could tear apart. Only faith, poetry, love, romance, can push aside that curtain and view and picture the supernal beauty and glory beyond...How dreary would be the world if there were no Santa Claus. It would be as dreary as if there were no Virginias."

In the years that followed, that editorial inspired songs, movies, stage plays, and even a cartoon. It is among the most-reprinted editorials in the history of American journalism.

83

A Book That

CHANGED CHRISTMAS

CHARLES DICKENS'S *A Christmas Carol* was published in 1834. It's a story of love and family and hope.

This Dickensian work was groundbreaking in many ways. Holidays were not popular or sentimentalized in 1830s England. Men worked 12 hours a day, six days a week, and children worked too, some as young as age 8. The character of Scrooge represented the Industrial Age, both in the US and England.

So Dickens used the power of story to make people take a hard look at their values. He encouraged a renewed focus on family and faith, giving and worship. Especially during the Christmas season.

It's impossible to say how much effect one book can have on popular culture, but after the publication of this classic, churches began holding special Christmas services. Families made the holiday a focus of their year.

The author's love for the season is evident in many of his famous quotations, including this one: "Happy, happy Christmas, that can win us back to the delusions of our childish days; recall to the old man the pleasures of his youth."

O Little Church
OF BETHLEHEM

EVEN PEOPLE WHO avoid church during the rest of the year often find their way to a service at Christmastime. If you had a choice of any church to attend for a Christmas service or Mass, you might pick the Church of the Nativity, located in historic Bethlehem. (And we are not talking Bethlehem, Pennsylvania, here. We mean old-school Bethlehem.) Located near the area known as Shepherds Field, the Church of the Nativity is the oldest church in the Holy Land, and many believe it to be the site of Jesus's birth. The door to this 1,700-year-old church is small and narrow, the lintel so low that attendees must, appropriately, kneel to enter.

However, this four-foot-high "Door of Humility" wasn't built to force people to bow. Rather, the design was intended to discourage looters on horseback and camelback after the Crusades.

The Church of the Nativity is one of the oldest churches in the world. It has survived invasions, regime changes, fires, earthquakes, and the 2002 siege of Bethlehem. During that conflict, armed Palestinians hid in the church for weeks, hoping to avoid Israeli forces.

Today, sadly, the church has fallen into disrepair. The roof is rotting, and water is dripping into the building, threatening some of the irreplaceable paintings and mosaics inside. Its condition has been deteriorating for decades. The church's resident clerics (representing the Greek Orthodox Church, the Armenian Orthodox Church, and the Franciscan order of the Roman Catholic Church) are jealous of one another's claims of custody, and they cannot agree on a plan of action for renovation.

A few years ago, several of the clerics were hospitalized after a fight broke out over who should dust the church's chandeliers and how the task should be done.

This church was built circa 330 CE by Constantine, the first Christian emperor of Rome. The building was devastated during the Samaritan rebellion of 529, but part of the original mosaic floor survived. Soon after the attack, Justinian, emperor of the Byzantine Empire, rebuilt the church in a larger and grander fashion. That structure from the 500s is, for the most part, the one that remains today.

At least for now.

DID YOU KNOW?

In 614 CE, the Persian army, who destroyed many churches during wars with Byzantium, spared the Church of the Nativity. The reason: It was a show of respect for one of the church's mosaics, which pictured the Magi wearing Persian attire.

Walt Disney,

THE US MARINES, AND THE TRUE SPIRIT OF CHRISTMAS

THE US MARINES do more than defend their country. Toys for Tots is a program run by the US Marine Corps Reserve, providing Christmas toys to children whose parents or guardians can't afford them. The program was launched in Los Angeles in 1947 by Major Bill Hendricks. Hendricks's wife, Diane, handcrafted a few dolls, which she wanted to donate to needy children. She asked her husband to find an agency to help her. When the major struck out, he received a command from his wife: "Start one!"

Major Hendricks and other Marines collected and distributed more than 5,000 toys to underprivileged children that year. The local success led the Marine commandant to direct that all Marine Reserve Sites implement a similar effort. Toys for Tots became a national program the next year (1948). Its goal: "To help bring the joy of Christmas and send a message of hope to America's less-fortunate children." Hendricks's civilian job was director of public relations at Warner Brothers Studios. Among his friends there was Walt Disney. As a favor to Hendricks, Disney designed the first Toys for Tots poster, featuring the mini three-car train that is the organization's official logo. Today, more than 16 million toys are distributed to 7 million kids.

86
A Sweet Truth
ABOUT CANDY CANES

FOR SOME, A CANDY CANE is just a minty holiday treat, but for others, this confection has special meaning. White candy canes were used to decorate Christmas trees and eaten as snacks for centuries. However, it wasn't until the early 1900s that some candymakers began adding red stripes. One of these confectioners explained how this addition made candy canes a sweet way to remind children of Christmas's religious significance:

- The white part of the candy cane represents Jesus's purity.
- The red stripes symbolize Jesus's death on the cross.
- The crook at the top looks like a shepherd's staff—a reminder that shepherds were the first to hear about the holy birth in Bethlehem.
- Turned upside down, the candy cane looks like the letter J, the first letter in Jesus.

The Annual Christmas Bonus

IF YOU'RE ONE of the fortunate workers who receive a Christmas bonus each year, you can thank F.W. Woolworth (as well as your boss, of course!). The department-store owner instituted what is believed to be the first Christmas bonus program back in 1899. Knowing how important Christmas was to his business, Woolworth wanted to make sure his workers approached the holiday season with a positive attitude. So he gave each employee a $5 bonus for each year of service. Even though he instituted a $25 cap on his program, it was a hefty sum for those times. (Twenty-five 1899 dollars equals about $771 today.)

That spirit of employee appreciation continues today. Consider FloraCraft, a 71-year-old family-owned manufacturer of foam products for the craft and floral industries. In 2018, FloraCraft owner Lee Schoenherr announced to his 200 employees that they would be sharing $4 million in Christmas bonus money, based on longevity. The average bonus was $15,000 to $20,000, but longtime employees received $60,000 or more.

"There were some smiles, there was cheering, and there were tears," Schoenherr said. "It brought tears to my eyes too, because this is the best Christmas I've ever had."

88

An Army
THAT FEEDS THE HUNGRY

IN THE WINTER OF 1891, Joseph McFee, a Salvation Army captain in San Francisco, offered a free Christmas dinner to his city's neediest people, numbering more than a thousand. But after making the offer, he had to find a way to finance his charitable effort. Night after night, he lay awake, worrying and praying. Then he recalled his days as a sailor in the British Navy. At Liverpool's Stage Landing, where boats would dock, some kind people had placed a large iron kettle, dubbed Simpson's Pot. As people passed by, they would toss in a coin or two to help the poor.

After securing the necessary permission, McFee placed a pot of his own at the foot of Market Street near the landing for the Oakland ferries. Beside the pot, he placed a sign imploring passers-by to "Keep the Pot Boiling." Soon he had enough money to feed the hundreds of people who might otherwise have gone hungry at Christmastime.

The kettle idea spread from the East Coast across the country. By 1897, the Salvation Army was providing more than 150,000 dinners for the needy across the United States. Today the organization assists more than 4.5 million people during the holiday season in the United States alone. And the kettles have gone international. You can find them from Korea to Japan to Chile to London.

89

Wanted:

A CIVIL CHRISTMAS

FOR CENTURIES IN WESTERN EUROPE, Christmas was a time of excess. In Britain, carolers called mummers roamed the streets, doing skits and singing songs that did not emphasize the season's holy elements. Even in church, people wore wild garb. Gambling during Christmas services was not uncommon. After church, some congregants would storm the homes of the well-off, pounding on doors and demanding their finest food and drink.

Imagine a combination of Mardi Gras and Halloween. That was Christmas of early-1800s England. Thus, devout Christians loathed the season. When America was colonized, some residents brought their bad holiday habits with them. In America's early days, Christmas meant drunken parties and rioting. That's why certain anti-Christmas laws remained in effect for decades. In 1828 New York, things became so bad that the city council formed a special police force devoted to handling unruly Christmas revelers. But law and order didn't work. It took a royal marriage to fix Christmas.

Prince Albert hailed from Germany, where Christmas was regarded as a sacred season. For families like Albert's, Christmas was a time of food, fellowship, togetherness, and honoring the Savior's birth. In 1840, Queen Victoria married Albert, who brought with him the reverent spirit and family focus of Christmas, the way it should be.

The World War 1
CHRISTMAS TRUCE

SOMETIMES THE CHRISTMAS SPIRIT shows up in unlikely places: like a World War I battlefield in Belgium.

On Christmas Eve 1914, German, British, and French troops put down their weapons in favor of a spontaneous holiday cease-fire.

The Germans are credited with starting the effort, as they decorated their trenches with Christmas trees and candles. Then they began singing favorite carols, like "Silent Night." British troops responded by singing "The First Noel." The Germans created signs reading "You No Fight, We No Fight." The Brits and French responded with signs of their own, saying simply, "Merry Christmas!"

Then, inspired by the spirit of the music and the season, the combatants ventured into "no man's land" (the blasted-out space between enemy trenches) and greeted one another with handshakes. They exchanged gifts, including cake, cognac, postcards, newspapers, and tobacco. They sang together and even played soccer. And they helped one another bury their dead.

Eventually, the generals ordered their armies to resume fighting. But even then, many of the soldiers on both sides obeyed the order only partially, firing bullets into the night sky rather than at one another. For a few moments, there was literal peace on earth.

Dreaming of a
WHITE CHRISTMAS?

LOTS OF AMERICANS DREAM of a white Christmas, but unless you live in Alaska, chances are that those dreams might not be realized. Based on averages over the past 30 years, the National Centers for Environmental Information lists the following contiguous United States cities that stand a 91 to a 100 percent chance of boasting at least an inch of snow on Christmas Day. They are...

- Jackson Hole, Wyoming
- Winthrop, Washington
- Mammoth Lakes, California
- Duluth, Minnesota
- Bozeman, Montana
- Marquette, Michigan
- Utica, New York
- Aspen, Colorado
- Crested Butte, Colorado
- International Falls, Minnesota

What are your city's chances of a white Christmas? Check out the National Oceanic Atmospheric Administration's interactive map. Enter "Probability of a White Christmas in the Continental US" in your search engine's browser bar. You'll be able to click on the map on that page to locate the spot you are wondering about.

Christmas Craziness

IF CHRISTMAS SEEMS like an especially crazy and frantic time of year—sheer bedlam, in fact—perhaps there is a good reason: The word *bedlam* is intrinsically linked to Christmas. In London's mid-thirteenth century was a monastery called St. Mary's of Bethlehem in honor of the biblical mother of Jesus.

Later, the name of the monastery was shortened to Beth'lem, and then later to simply Bedlam (and, according to some sources, Bedlem). In the early 1400s, Bedlam was turned from a monastery into a house of detention for the criminally insane.

So, when it seems as if Christmastime is sheer bedlam, now you know the (possible) reason why.

I Break for Christmas

A COLLEGE STUDENT was taking her last final exam before Christmas break. Midway through the test, she became frustrated with its difficulty. Finally, in exasperation, she wrote, "Only God knows the answers to these questions! Merry Christmas!"

With that, she turned in the exam. After the holiday break, she received her graded test back, with this note from the professor: "God gets an A. You get an F! Happy New Year!"

> "IT IS CHRISTMAS EVERY TIME
> YOU LET GOD LOVE OTHERS
> THROUGH YOU...YES, IT IS
> CHRISTMAS EVERY TIME YOU
> SMILE AT YOUR BROTHER AND
> OFFER HIM YOUR HAND."
>
> —MOTHER TERESA

'Tis the Season

FOR COMMERCIALS

AD AGENCIES often put forth their best efforts during the Christmas buying season, a tradition that precedes the advent of television.

The world's first "singing commercial" aired on the radio on Christmas Eve, 1926, for Wheaties cereal. The four male singers, eventually known as the Wheaties Quartet, sang a jingle touting the cereal's benefits. The Wheaties Quartet, composed of an undertaker, a bailiff, a printer, and a businessman, performed the song for the next six years at $6 per singer per week.

The commercials were a resounding success. Some advertising experts credit the campaign with saving Wheaties, which was a failing brand at the time. During the 1920s, General Mills seriously considered dropping the cereal due to poor sales. But when company execs realized that almost 60 percent of all Wheaties sales were coming from Minneapolis-St. Paul (the only area featuring the commercial at the time), they took the Wheaties Quartet national.

The result: People across the country bought the cereal, which is today one of the world's best-known and most enduring brands. And it all started with a Christmas Eve jingle.

There Are No People
LIKE SNOW PEOPLE

IF AMERICA HAS a "snowman/snowwoman capital," it might be Bethel, Maine. In 1999, Jim Sysko and 60 volunteers from the Bethel area built Angus, the world's largest snowman. Angus stood 113 feet, 7 inches tall, topping the previous record snowman by 17 feet. Angus's estimated weight: 9 million pounds.

Not to be outdone, another group of volunteers from Bethel (and surrounding towns) created a snowwoman who stood just over 122 feet high. More than 13 million pounds of snow were used to build Olympia, who was just a few feet shorter than the Statue of Liberty. The project took a month to complete.

A few more details about Olympia, who was named in honor of Olympia Snowe, a US Senator from Maine:

- Her eyelashes were constructed from eight pairs of skis.

- Her fleece hat was 48 feet wide.

- Her nose was eight feet long and was constructed from chicken wire and painted cheesecloth.

- Her lips were crafted from five red car tires.

- Her scarf was 130 feet long.

- Three five-foot-wide truck tires served as buttons on her "outfit."
- Two 30-foot spruce trees served as her arms.

If you'd like to create your own perfect snow creation at Christmastime, here are a few tips from the experts:

1. Build in a shady spot.

2. If the snow is too powdery, sprinkle it with water from a hose or watering can.

3. Flatten the top of a ball of snow before adding another on it.

4. Get help hefting the middle section of your creation; it can be heavier than you think.

5. Pack reinforcing snow around the base, waist, and neck to help keep your snow person (or creature) stable.

6. Get creative with accent materials. Chow Mein noodles, for example, can make a great spiky hairdo.

"A SNOW DAY LITERALLY
AND FIGURATIVELY
FALLS FROM THE SKY,
UNBIDDEN, AND SEEMS LIKE
A THING OF WONDER."

—SUSAN ORLEAN

96

Does Your Christmas

BRING HOME THE BACON?

FOR MANY PEOPLE, Christmas is a season for reflection and reassessment. That has been true for a long time. In old England, for example, it was a time for couples to consider "bringing home the bacon." However, in the 1600s the phrase had nothing to do with earning a living and much to do with marital harmony. During this era, the Christmas season would inspire couples to consider, "How have we done this year?"

If a couple was willing to swear upon the King James Bible that they had not engaged in a marital spat for the past year, the church awarded them a side of bacon. And that's bound to spice up anyone's Christmas.

Of course, trying to find a logical connection between a hunk of cured pork and marital bliss is like trying to catch a greased pig. Sometimes love defies logic.

Love

A Very Chinese Christmas

THIS BOOK, WE HOPE, provides a window to how Christmas is celebrated in the United States as well as in parts of Europe. But what about countries not directly connected to Christmas? What about China, for example?

As you might guess, Christmas in China is much like any other day. Kids attend school, people head to work, and all businesses and shops are open. China is a non-religious state, and Christmas was banned at one point (along with Christianity itself).

A careful observer can see elements of Christmas in China, especially in its larger cities, but it's more like Valentine's Day than a day with religious or spiritual meaning. (Keep in mind that only 1 percent of the Chinese population is Christian.)

In China, you are more likely to spend Christmas Day with friends than family, and you celebrate by going to the movies or doing some shopping. Sometimes sweethearts spend the day together. Perhaps that's why Christmas Eve is China's biggest shopping day. But maybe more people in the world's most populous country are discovering the wonder that is Christmas.

As Pure as the Driven
ASBESTOS?

UNFORTUNATELY, much of the information shared on social media is unreliable, if not deliberately misleading, whether it's about Christmas, cures for the common cold, or the joys of cow-tipping.

However, just as a broken clock is correct twice a day, sometimes social media posts are strange *and* true.

During the 2017 holiday season, an image of a box labeled "Asbestos: Pure White Fire Proof Snow" began popping up on social media. Savvy readers quickly dubbed the picture a hoax. After all, who would purchase artificial snow made from a well-known carcinogen?

As it turns out, lots of people during the first half of the twentieth century, when asbestos was widely employed as Christmas decor. Consumers loved its white and fluffy texture and appearance. Of course, they didn't know it was a major risk factor in an aggressive form of cancer called mesothelioma.

According to the website asbestosproservices.com, "Asbestos was once marketed as artificial snow and sprinkled on trees and wreaths and ornaments. Although those products have not been produced for many years, the oldest decorations that were passed down from one generation to the next may have small amounts of asbestos."

Perhaps the most famous "asbestos snow scene" appears in *The Wizard of Oz*, the 1939 classic film starring Judy Garland. There is a scene in the movie where snow, made from asbestos, falls on Dorothy and her friends, awakening them from a spell cast by the Wicked Witch of the West.

Of course, the artificial snow products for sale today bear labels like "safe" and "nontoxic," but you should still read all labels carefully, just in case.

This Christmas,

YOUR ESCAPE IS IN THE CARDS

UNITED STATES TROOPS and playing cards share a long history. Military deployment sometimes means passing long hours between missions or other responsibilities, and various card games have helped servicemen and women pass the time for many years.

But there is at least one case of the cards being more than a time killer. During World War II, playing card manufacturer Bicycle teamed up with US and British intelligence agencies to create an unusual deck of cards. The cards pulled apart when moistened, revealing a piece of a secret escape map designed to help downed pilots and captured soldiers find their way back to Allied territory. Once all the map pieces were revealed, they could be assembled to produce the full escape map.

Decks of these special cards were provided to POWs in Europe as part of Christmas parcels assembled by the Red Cross. Because playing cards were omnipresent during wartime, Axis captors paid little attention.

Did the ploy work? Yes. The cards helped at least 32 POWs escape from the infamous prison camp at Colditz Castle in Saxony, a site that specialized in housing POWs who had escaped from other facilities. All told, the cards were at the center of more than 300 escape attempts, though no one knows how many of them were successful.

The Gift of a Wombat

IF THERE IS A PERSON on your Christmas gift list who is notoriously hard to shop for, the World Wildlife Fund might have a solution for you

Even the man or woman who has everything probably does not have a wombat. That's where the WWF comes in. For a fee (ranging from $25 to $100, depending on the adoption package), you can virtually adopt a wombat, the plump marsupial found in the forests and mountains of Tasmania and southeastern Australia.

These nocturnal herbivores, who live on grasses and roots, are a threatened species due to hunting. Farmers shoot them as a nuisance, while others are killed for their fur or simply for sport.

The "wombat adoption fees" support conservation efforts.

If a wombat doesn't seem like the right symbolic gift for someone on your list, the WWF offers a variety of virtual adoption options, including meerkats, slow lorises, and narwhals.

A Degree from Santa U?

HAVE YOU EVER WONDERED how the Santa Clauses you encounter at department stores, malls, parades, or other events *become* Santas? Is there special training, a Santa University?

The answer is yes, and the best-known US Santa training program is located in Colorado, not the North Pole.

The Noerr Programs, an Arvada, Colorado–based effort, has created Santa University, which trains and assigns Santas to 225 shopping centers and other sites in 38 states.

According to Dan Short, an author and veteran Santa, Santa University teaches students about beard bleaching and general care, hygiene, costume maintenance, and makeup. Santas are taught the importance of being punctual, polite, and patient. They learn how to respond to questions from kids and their parents (and from the media), and how to deal with the inevitable crisis situations.

Being Santa means more than relying on instinct. Imagine needing to hold kids of various ages, religions, sizes—and with a variety of physical or other challenges. Students also learn basic sign language and Spanish phrases to help them interact with as many children as possible.

A typical class consists of about 80 Santas. And they do more than learn. They create care packages for Operation Santa's Stocking, which provides aid to the armed forces and children's ministries.